About the Author

For over three decades, Carmel Cayouf has fulfilled high-level executive management positions. He gained vast experience and skills in organisational management, both general and logistic, in which he successfully developed and practiced various methods and concepts of management, for which he gained recognition. For the last ten years, has been an entrepreneur and investor and highly involved in the domain of "self development", which helped and supported him in his work and businesses. His vast experience from years of practical experience and practice is reflected in his concept of the "Methodical Approach's" impact on our success and goals' achievements.

On the Path to Wealth

Carmel Cayouf

On the Path to Wealth

Olympia Publishers
London

www.olympiapublishers.com
OLYMPIA PAPERBACK EDITION

Copyright © Carmel Cayouf 2024

The right of Carmel Cayouf to be identified as author of this work has been asserted in accordance with sections 77 and 78 of the Copyright, Designs and Patents Act 1988.

All Rights Reserved

No reproduction, copy or transmission of this publication may be made without written permission.
No paragraph of this publication may be reproduced, copied or transmitted save with the written permission of the publisher, or in accordance with the provisions of the Copyright Act 1956 (as amended).

Any person who commits any unauthorised act in relation to this publication may be liable to criminal prosecution and civil claims for damage.

A CIP catalogue record for this title is available from the British Library.

ISBN: 978-1-80439-924-8

The information in this book has been compiled by way of general guidance only. Neither the author nor the publisher shall be liable or responsible for any loss or damage allegedly arising from any information or suggestion in this book. Examples brought in this book are the author's imagination. Any resemblance to actual persons situations, living or dead is purely coincidental.

First Published in 2024

Olympia Publishers
Tallis House
2 Tallis Street
London
EC4Y 0AB

Printed in Great Britain

"Remember that your real wealth can be measured not by what you have, but by what you are."

Napoleon Hill – Think and Grow Rich

Prologue

"Accomplishment will prove to be a journey, not a destination."
(Dwight D. Eisenhower)

Extraordinary accomplishments throughout our history were and are led by persons who dared to vision, think and take action. The common thread that binds those extraordinary individuals together through time and space is their courage to take action on a dream they had, despite any risks or reservations they were facing. A path to success and wealth is a journey. A journey that has a destination which is beyond the here and now that we are living, and that has a profound impact on the reality of ourselves, the ones we love, and even on the ones we don't personally know. One accomplishment along our path is a jumping step to the next one. The constant growing and improving of our lives is not a one-time accomplishment, and it is fuelled and ignited by our own ambitions, led from our beliefs and inner resoluteness.

In this book, you will embark on a journey. A journey along the milestones of the path to success and wealth. This book will lay down to you the needed faculties and qualities needed to transform your life into the exceptional life you desire. The ideas in this book are not fictional nor philosophical, they are proven facts and concepts that shared by advanced researches of the mind in the last decades, as well as leading executive management methods and doctrines.

As you will see in this book, I find approaching life's goals and achievements similar to approaching a management of an organisation or a company as quite logical and beneficial. Adopting a **Methodical Approach** and **executive management thinking** focuses our energies and efforts in a certain set of actions in order to achieve a desired reality for our lives. I urge you not to dismiss the analogy from a place of uncomfortableness, but rather to examine it in light of the tools and ideas this book offers you.

During my long years of experience in executive management, entrepreneurship and self-development, I found that methodical thinking and executions, while observing the facts as they are, without giving any added or sentimental value to them, combined with a clear goal that is backed up with a plan and with an empowering mindset, is the ultimate formula for success and wealth. This secret is good and valid for both big plans and small plans, big goals and small goals. Once you adopt these techniques and way of thinking and practice them, you will find that they become normal in your life and part of who you are, helping you to achieve the desired life you dream of.

Don't delay your actions and charge on your life's dream right away, for the deeds of today will define your tomorrow.

Chapter One
Where Does It All Begin?

Did you ever consider the difference between **wealthy people** and **poor people?**

I have struggled with this question for years…
What makes people wealthy, and what makes them poor (taking in consideration they didn't win the lottery or had a rich relative that left them huge amounts of money)?

Is it hard work?
Well, we all work hard and give our best in what we do, but it doesn't seem to bring us the results we are hoping for, while there are people (you may know one or two of them) that are not working that hard and making big amounts of money.

Is it higher education?
Well, they are a lot of very educated people out there with several degrees hanging on their wall and they are still poor, whilst other not so high educated are making millions and living their dream.

Is it that we are not smart enough?
I can assure you that you and I are way smarter than a lot of people who are making millions.

So, what is it?

Answering this question is not an easy task. After all, there are a lot of factors involved in a person achievements and results. However, if we could, for a moment, look beyond the facade of things, beyond the obvious, and if we were to examine much closer success and failure stories, we surely would find some factors that are in a much broader scales than other and are, in a way or another, shared between all of them.

It would be superficial to allocate one reason to success or to failure. Those are results that are driven from a process of some kind, either professional, business, personal or shared. The dynamic of the process, by definition, is constructed from many ***"moving parts"***, which in their turn, can have a dynamic of their own and in some cases cloud the main process or even set its fate.

Understanding the ***"moving parts"*** in the process is crucial, since it can give us the sense of importance of each component, and when I talk about the importance, I solely mean, the ***impact force*** of that component on the desired result being achieved. Once we understand those two things: *moving parts* have their own dynamic and each has relatively different *score of impact*, then we are ready to analyse any process and understand or identify the common laws that drive the result of our process, while giving us the skill of unbiased observation that is imperative for our ability to take corrective actions and drive through to our desired *goal*.

Now, that we understand how a process is built and in what dynamic it exists, we need to understand that a process does not exist ***on its own***. A process has no right of existing if it's not in order to achieve a goal. A goal can be anything we decide on. If we were to decide we want to go to a restaurant, which is the goal, then the process of preparing ourselves, making reservations, dressing up and driving there is the *action chain* that will bring us to our goal. Of course, a goal can be as simple as going to a restaurant or as important and life changing as *to be wealthy*. In the *skeletal essence* of it, the process exists in order to *achieve a result*.

What does that mean?

It means that *the process* is a secondary phase that includes a chain of actions, and it's not the primary one thus, it does not have the right of existence on its own.

If the process is the secondary phase and its existence is defined by a higher hierarchy, then what is the primary phase?

Firstly, we need to decide on our G*oal*. What is it that we are out to achieve? Where do we want to arrive? What do we want to change or create? The *Goal* is our destination, and like everything in life, each destination has its set of rules and characteristics. These are imperative to identify, for they are the key of understanding and carrying out properly the follow up steps. *(Further discussion about goals in the next chapter)*.

OK, so we have a Goal, what now?

Nothing can be achieved without a *Plan*. In order for us to start a journey, we need to set a destination, and we need to plan the route. You don't go in a taxi and just tell the driver "*Drive*", "*Where?*" he will ask! Where do you want to go? It is a simple question that we take for granted and understand it in everyday life, but sometimes, ignore it when it's about *life itself*!

A plan is a declaration of both intention and commitment. Since once you devised a plan and identified the landmarks and actions needed to achieve the success of the plan, you put your thoughts, intentions and amount of energy in this devise. Needless to point out that the more we are thinking and allocating energy to this plan, the more we become emotionally attached, we start to see ourselves in that place when the plan fruited the desired result and achieved the impact it has on our lives. This involvement creates an inner drive that will be the fuel for our upcoming process.

I see a lot of people thinking of a result they want, or a situation they want to create, and from there they *jump* into a process! This process is bound to have major setbacks in the best case and total failure in the most probable case. And why is that? In essence and simply put, this person in question did not evaluate nor did he analyse deeply enough the actions needed in order and in importance *(score of impact)* on his way to take action.

So, a *goal* alone is not enough. You need a *plan* to achieve it, and a plan alone is an idea that has no physical grounds, so, now, you need a chain of **actions** *(process)* in order to carry your plan out.

Let's recap for a moment…

A G*oal* is an ambition, destination or situation we want to achieve. A *plan* is a road map that describes the *way* to that destination. It's the art of identifying the stages, landmarks, actions and relationships needed in order to achieve the goal. A process is the *physical and actual activity* of taking action, in order to materialise the stages in our plan. Since we talked about the fact that the process is built out of many *moving parts* – which is the nature of the physical entity – we need to evaluate and analyse those parts in the sense of urgency, costs and most importantly the importance *(the score of the impact they have on achieving the plan)*. Each component has its own relative impact in achieving the steps of the plan, which in their turn, if they are achieved successfully, will bring about the fulfillment of the desired goal. We plan from UP – DOWN and we execute from DOWN – UP. Each successful task or sub-process we have, is another step closer to achieving the plan and ultimately the goal.

Someone might say, *"Well, the concept is not strange to me, I practically work by the same method, but still, I don't achieve the results I want."*

This is the thing… this argument takes us back to the beginning, what is it that makes the difference?

I wish the answer resided just in the concept I laid out above: setting a goal, devising a plan and starting a process. No doubt those steps are crucial to success, but they can't stand alone.

Those are external factors that are technical in essence, and can be even delegated in some cases.

The truth is that the answer to the question is much more eluding and complex. The idea of a technical answer is almost insulting, and it's no way near the scope of factors involved.

The inner factor that is called the *mindset* and the conviction of our achievement that is called *belief*, among other factors, are main players we ought to take in consideration while weighing the question of success and failure *(Further discussion about goals in the next chapters).*

This book is discussing *wealth*[1] as a goal, therefore, there are additional "technical" factors that will be discussed further. The **combinations** of the *ideas* brought in the book will give you a broader, and hopefully, indexed observation on the question at hand.

---

[1] *Even though the main discussion in the book is wealth making, in my experience, the ideas and principals brought here are valid for any domain of goals you desire, with few adjustments of the contexts.

Chapter Two
Setting up Goals

A ***Goal***, as discussed above, is the *"end result"* we want to *achieve*. It's the *destination* of our *journey* and a step in arriving to our *vision*[2].

A *goal* is a *strategical pivot* that achieving it, will strategically change an existing reality in such a profound way that it imposes the new reality as *the default version,* or creating a new reality or situation that is needed for us *(in the case of this book)* to live a life of our choice and have the things we desire. It is also a very important and crucial step to ultimately live the life of our *vision*.

In *this book,* we are discussing *personal success and wealth creating*. But, the idea of a *goal* and of a *vision* as brought here, is valid and crucial in any business or a life plan that we choose, that is to say, it's valid for our personal life, our professional life and for organisational purposes.

Opposing to common thinking, a goal can be big *(very big)* or it can be small. In fact, most of us set goals and achieve them each day without thinking about them in an intimidating way. Since we take them for granted, and we make them on daily bases almost on automatic mode, that we don't give them the

---

[2] *A "vision" is the ultimate and most extensive part of our journey and the ultimate "Why" that in its name we take an action. Achieving the vision of our lives is always a combined effort of several goals that need to add up together. In this book, we will not discuss the vision, and we will concentrate on the goals and plan of action.*

significant meaning in the context of our abilities, and sadly, sometimes even *mock* them and doing so, we are creating a negative anchor in our subconscious mind as for our abilities and self-esteem.

Obviously, I don't know the background or abilities of each reader, but consider this an example to demonstrate my point. If you are a parent and a job holding person, then each day in the morning you have a goal. You want to drop your children at school at eight and be at your job at nine. This is a goal that requires a chain of actions in order to achieve it. You will need to wake up at six-half (depending on your location, number of kids and so on), to wake your children up, make sure they wash up, dress and take their books, you will need to prepare yourself as well, make breakfast, eat and go out of the house. On your way to the school and work you need to drive your car or take the right public transportation in such manner that ensures your arrival at the designated hour as defined in your goal. Some would think, it's a simple task, and it's not a goal, nothing is complicated here. Well, this example is the definition of a goal. You set a reality that you want, you decide and define a timeline and most importantly, you achieve it by the combined efforts of several small tasks in a ***methodical*** manner and order. While for you this goal can seem too easy and not worthy, I can assure you, that for a lot of other folks it is not an easy task. As a matter of fact, some would prefer doing a physical activity and not to try to carry this goal out!

The main difference between those who find it easy and routine and those who don't, is the *familiarity* that comes with it and the *normality* of it in our lives. Once it's a *habit*, it becomes easy, and once we are *skilled* in executing it, it becomes a small matter and vice versa the same. We will get into those ideas in the next chapters, and I will explain further what I mean.

Going back to setting the *goal* – We understand now, that a goal is built of several *tasks* or *actions,* that a *combined execution* of them together, will achieve our *"end result".* We also understand, that we are all achieving goals, every day, without even thinking about them, since they are *normal* in our lives.

I would totally agree that there is a difference between the *goals*. As I said earlier, a *Goal* can be big or small, have three required actions in its process or twenty, require just our own efforts or joined efforts with others. *This difference does not define the goal.* This is a technicality that points out the complexity of it, nothing more.

Furthermore, every *goal* is *strategical* in the sense of its influence on the outcome of our reality in its *timeframe*. In the example above, arriving on time to school and work, is a *strategical pivot.* Should we fail to achieve it, there will be consequences for the rest of our day, in the best case, and sometimes for longer. Consider the stress, the argument with your manager that will leave you feeling down all day, the missing of a meeting or an important work that you will need to catch up with, and so on!

How do we determine our Goals?

This is a good question. The goals we set to ourselves reflect the dreams we have, and the way we want to live our lives. Setting up a goal can be fulfilling as much as it can be frustrating. It really depends on our position in life and our abilities, but not only. It also depends on our inner strength, beliefs, *paradigm* and self-confidence.[3]

    I, for one, am a very big supporter of ***"Dream Big"*** and set ***"Big Goals"***. Goals, that we believe in and resonate with, have enormous positive impact on our lives. They give us a significance, a ***"Why"*** for our actions, and they drive us to constant improvement and excellency in what we do and how we live. They encourage us and push us forward. On the other hand, if our goals do not resonate with who we are and with our ***values***[4] in life, they can become frustrating and a cause of low self-esteem.

    That is why it is ***imperative*** to ***know who we are***, what are the things that make us smile and feel full of life, and what define us as individuals. It would seem obvious that we would know who we are, wouldn't it? The fact is, that it is ***not*** that obvious. People tend to define their happiness and themselves by the things that they lack in their lives, rather than the things that they have.

    Knowing one's self is a crucial set point from where we need to start. This point cannot be defined by ***external factors.*** It is the essence of who we are, our inner truth and being!

    For example, if a person is in lack of a true relationship, he or she will jump to the conclusion that finding their soul-mate and having a perfect relationship is their true being, and thus their Goal in life. Another, may have financial difficulties, and think

---

[3] *A paradigm is the set of beliefs and habits imbedded in our subconscious mind and determine our way of behaviour and the way we see the world and value things. The paradigm is created in us by the age of seven and it's the result of our environment and experiences till that age and forward.*
when we talk about 'values', we are not referring to the values in the meaning of morals or right or wrong, but in the meaning of importance and focus of aspects in our lives (like making money, family, children, self-development and etc.).

that if he would have been wealthy, his life would be perfect. Mind you, I am not stating that those goals are not *worthy* or they are not *noble*, they are!

As long that those goals resonate with the true values of the person in question, they are just right for him, but, once they are driven from the point of view of lack, they are not!

You see, our goals need to come from a source of *abundance* not *lack*, from the source of *love* not *need* and from the source of **belief** not **influence**. In short, they need to come from **inside** us **out** rather than from **outside** of us **in**. What is coming from inside of us has an energetic drive that is **fuelled** *by our ambitions and convictions*, while, what is coming from the outside, is **confronted** *with our ambitions and convictions.*

So, setting our goals in life need to be in alignment with our true being, it needs to reflect our *true desires,* and it needs to be generated from *inside* of us not imported from the *outside* as an *influence*. Our goals need to *reflect* the answer to a big *"**Why**"* in our lives and the *bigger the "Why"* is, *the bigger the goal* should be!

Next question that can arise would be as the following:

What if my big goal in life does not resonate with my beliefs and values? What if, I *consciously* understand the impact of achieving that goal would have on my life and the lives of my loved ones, but, *unconsciously*, my beliefs are sabotaging my efforts of achievements?

Firstly, I can assure you that, as a *starter point,* almost *no one* has the perfect conditions in order to achieve their goals. We all need to go through some kind of a journey in our lives, some more, some less, but nevertheless, we all have to take this journey in order to achieve our goals.

The first good news would be the fact that one recognises his or her *strengths* and *weaknesses* in light of the *goal*. The second good news is that our mind is so complex and evolved, that we actually have the ability to change it. No doubt this process takes some time and efforts, but once you make a decision to stick to the process, have the commitment and the techniques, you will be amazed how things will start shifting in your mind, first, on the *"thought"* level and after that, on the *"physical"* level.

Napoleon Hill, in his book, *"Think and Grow Rich"* said, and I quote *"what the mind can conceive and believe, the mind can achieve."* Meaning that, whatever we believe and are convinced in, we can achieve. The belief is not on the conscious level. It's much deeper, and it resides in our *subconscious* that has no filters of acceptance, and its main role is to *"protect us"* from any inconvenience or excessive energy use. Once the subconscious mind accepts an idea as a reality, and as a needed *"code"* not a *"virus"*, it will create the needed *"protocols"* in our mind to make it normal, and to implement it in our *programme (paradigm)*, so it would not consume energy and become set on *auto-pilot mode*.

In the next chapters, we will deepen in this idea of our *programme* and talk about techniques and methods that can help us to manipulate our subconscious mind.

Let's recap:

A goal is a reflection of the envisioned life we want to live or at least, a part of it. Living a life without a goal is like driving a car with no destination. So, it is crucial that we get costumed to the art of setting goals and having references in life from the point in which we are now, to the point we want to arrive to.

No matter how big or small the *goal* is, it would be in need of *definition* in terms of *timeframe*, *actions* and *resources*. Each one of us has his own set of *values* that *drives him* in life, and his own *programme* that determines the way he or she *looks at life*.

A goal that is set in a contradiction with our values or beliefs will surely be fated to failure and cause pain and frustration. It is imperative to match our goals to our values and beliefs or to change them to match our goals. Both are valid, depending where you want to go in life. There is no judgment and no right or wrong, it's a journey that each takes according to his destination in life.

Chapter Three
The Action Plan

After understanding the process of *goal* setting and defining the *conditions* in which we set the goals, now is the time to talk about the *action plan* of how to *achieve* our goal.

I want to start with two very important statements that, in my opinion, will put your mind in ease while reading this chapter:

1. A plan of action is a *base for change*, meaning that your plan *can be changed* along the way depending on your *learning process and experiences*.

2. You don't need to wait till you have *a hundred per cent plan* with hermetical closures of all ends in order to start your execution. The importance of its being a *road map* and *identifying gaps* in our way, is the main *contribution* of the plan.

Those ideas will be discussed further in this chapter.

When coming to defining our *plan of action*, first we need to start in a *process of evaluation*. *Evaluation* of the *goal* we set up to achieve, of our *current state* both *mentally* and *physically* and *evaluation* of our *skills* and *knowledge* that are *needed* to achieve our goals. It is senseless to determine upon a plan, with no proper evaluation of those aspects. Each, in its own turn and character, sheds a *different light* on the actions needed, the timeframe of the plan, the resources and the acquiring of knowledge needed. The evaluation process is a *higher resolution* and a more *focused* and *direct continuance* of the *methodology* discussed in the previous chapter.

Once we finished the evaluation process, and we can clearly state our strengths, weaknesses and risks along the way, we can then, devise a plan that is *comprehensive,* in the sense of taking in consideration all *conditions for success*. It is very important to determine the origin point of the plan, the *timeline* and the *conditions of success* for each component of it.

The real power of the plan lies in its ability to *integrate* different aspects and natures of actions in a **methodical** manner and *timeframe*.

To start your plan, you need to *categorize* and write down all the points from your *evaluation* process. Categorizing means *organising* the points in *groups*. These groups are the *summary* of the *fields* that you need to deal with in your plan. Categorizing in groups makes it much easier to *relate* the *actions* to a specific *group* and thus, to *evaluate* their *contributions* in filling the *gaps* in that specific area. It is very possible, that some actions or points we revealed in our evaluation process, are actually connected and *directly influencing more than one category.* Mark those down. Those will become the *bottlenecks* in your plan and the *pivot points* in the execution, since more than one path of our plan is conditioned by them and depends on their fulfillment.

The categories that we determine are driving from our evaluation process. But most common categories are the following:
1. Financial.
2. Skills and Knowledge.
3. Relationship and Community.
4. Legal and Administrative.
5. Technical.
6. Outsourcing *(to an external specialist)*.

Let's examine an example:

Let's presume that in order to achieve your goal you will need a *working website* with a *merchant gateway* in order to accept online payments via credit cards. In essence, this is a *Technical* step and task, that if you know how to do it, and what is expected from you, then it's *"stand alone"* task that needs to be *integrated* in the plan according to its *timeline* and the *timeframe* that it will take you to finish it. *However*, if this task is a new one to you or you don't know how to fully make it, then you will need to *acquire* the right *knowledge and skill* in order to be able to make it. Now, the *timeframe* of building a site *automatically* got longer and now, it depends on *another action under another category (Skills and Knowledge)*. This becomes a *critical point in the process*. Let's go a bit further and complicate things a bit more, and say for example, that you haven't *registered* your company yet, or you don't have all the *legal documents* for your activity. In this case, you will not be able to set up your *merchant gateway,* and your website cannot be fully *functional*. Now, the simple task of building a website is suddenly *depending* on two *critical points* that, in their turns, are *"stand alone"* actions *connected* to *other categories*.

Firstly, you need to take care of those two steps before you're going to be able to have a fully functional website. The fact that those actions are *determining* the *existence* of the *website*, makes them *critical junctions* and in some cases *pivot points* in the process. If the *execution* of those tasks *becomes harder* and more demanding of *time, energy* and *money,* and influencing the *advancement* of the *whole plan*, then they become *bottlenecks* and need to be *flagged and* dealt with in a *focused* manner, understanding their *impact* on the *successful execution* of the plan as a whole.

Of course, you can choose to *outsource* this task to an external specialist, but then, you will need to take in consideration other *categories* that are *integrated* in the process such as *Financials* – since you need to pay for the service you are getting, *Relationships* – since you need to find and contract that specialist and of course, *Technical* because of the nature of the task, and the fact that it's conditioning the *functionality* of your site.

So, now you see how important is the categorizing of the conclusion brought up by the *evaluation* process. Of course, this is just one example to illustrate the **methodology** of devising a plan. It may seem intimidating, but trust me, once you have the evolution process finished and categorized your tasks, it will all *fall in place* and be much clearer how to *advance*.

This is the power of the **Methodical Process**. A logical *methodology* in any process is a sign of *focus*, since you can correctly *identify* the *connections* and *influences* of each *component* in the plan.

The next step of your plan is to build the *roadmap*, clearly *identifying* the *critical junction*s and *bottlenecks*. The *roadmap* is built like a *diagram* in which *each task* is connected to its category and *all categories* are connected to the *goal*. Naturally, not all *blocks* on the *roadmap* carry the same *importance* and *impact* on our goal achievement, neither will they carry the same *complexity* in their *execution*. This, in turn, will be another *indicator* for you where to *focus* your *energies,* after identifying those tasks that carry with the *biggest impact* on your *results* and therefore, you are able to *assign importance and priority* to them in the *execution* of the plan.

Now, you have a plan! You have a route in which you know

which turn you need to take, what junctions you need to cross, the timeline you are operating in, and what priorities you need to assign in order to arrive to your destination.

At this point, I'd like to go back to the beginning of this chapter, and elaborate the two *calming statements* I opened with.

In order to discuss those points, first I need you to understand that the *process of formulating* an *action plan* carries in it both *opportunity* and *risk*.

The obvious opportunity is the fact that the *methodical* process will surely expose you to valuable information about the things you need to accomplish in your path to achieving your goal. I cannot even start to stress the *huge importance and impact of this fact upon your success*.

On the other hand, in this process, we are exposed to an *eluding risk* that can seriously *jeopardize* the execution of our plan! Unfortunately, many people fall in the trap of this *eluding risk*. In many cases, people tend to perfect their plan to the smallest details, causing *procrastination* and *delays* in execution. In most cases, this process of *procrastination* is hidden from their conscious thinking. It is not caused by intended action or decision. Nevertheless, the result is the same.

To prevent you from falling in this trap, you will need to understand, and accept the fact that an action plan is a reference. It is most certainly not God's giving word on earth, especially in its low *hierarchy* components, but also in the objectives **(not the Goal)**. It can be *Adjusted and Changed* along the way, depending on new *opportunities* that serve your vision and goal. You will need **flexibility** *of the* **thought** *and* **execution**, in order to be able to identify and evaluate your situation on each point of the way. You need to be opened to *new ideas* that *emerge* from the **dynamics** of the process. Those opportunities and ideas can certainly be *much better* and more *contributing* to your *goal*, but were *unknown* to you prior your intensive activity in the execution of your plan. This is a *dynamic* process with many **moving parts** that have a *'life'* of their own, and are driven by the energy of your activity.

When we say the *action plan* is a *base of change*, we basically understand that our evaluation of the process led us to decide upon a plan. By all means, this plan *should and will* bring us to the *achievement* of our *goal,* which means, that its *methodology* and *tasks* are capable of delivering the results *desired*. Being as it is, the *action plan* is indeed a worthy **reference** to which we need to go back, over and over, and *measure* our results and advancement. Therefore, it is important to understand the need of a constant *evaluation* of the action plan in order to redefine *(if needed)* our *bottlenecks* and *critical points* as well as *identifying* the components that are *interfering* with the proper execution of it.

This action of reference, in turn, will *expose* us to new *possibilities* and *ideas*, *opportunities* and *shortcuts* that are revealed to us by the *dynamics* of our *activity,* and the *evolvement* and *learning process* we are undertaking along the way. As long as those insights don't interfere with other paths of our plan, and have a clear advantage in our favour of achieving our goal, it would be very wise to consider them with an open mind, and if necessary, adjust our plan accordingly.

The plan of action is *not a goal* by itself. It's the *mean* which we use to achieve the *desired goal,* so the importance of its stability is **relative** in any *giving point*.

Once you have your roadmap, and in order to avoid the hidden traps, you need to start taking action right away.

Chapter Four
Wrapping Up

Up until now, we covered the very *foundations* of our process, highlighting the *insights* and *techniques* of how to **methodically** create a *plan of action*.

This was the base of it all. The next chapters are to support you achieving your goals and sticking to your plan, by integrating certain *ideas, principles and habits* in the execution of the plan *(and in life in general)* to support your success!

In this chapter, I will lay down, yet another example for you to *fully comprehend* the process of devising a *plan of action*. I will be *expanding* some ideas brought earlier, and explain the *dynamics* of the process, the *flexibility of thought and execution* you must acquire, as well as the *resilience* you need to equip yourself with.

It is important to pay attention to this chapter, since it will introduce you to some of the *ideas* coming up later on, and it will act as a *bridge* to them.

As we discussed, a *goal* is something that you *want* to *achieve* in life, and that you *believe* achieving it will have a positive *impact* on the quality of your life and your happiness. Of course, our lives do not summarize up in just one *goal,* and just as we have talked about big *goals* and small goals, we can easily talk about *long term goals* and *short-term goals.*

It is quite normal that one *goal* is a *step towards* another bigger *goal,* as it's just normal that a goal is *definitive*. This doesn't matter, and has no consequence on the process itself.

It can also be that we have *several goals* that are *combining* together to serve a bigger goal – we mentioned this at the beginning and referred to it as a *vision*.

Once you set your *goal*, and you know that it *resonates* with your *being*, you need to start treating it as *already achieved,* and build the *resilience of the thought* around it. This is very important for it's going to give you the *motivation* and *drive* to start your process.

Once you start *believing* in your *goal* and treat it as an absolute *reality*, your *mind* will find you the ways and the insights that are needed, to *particulate* your *plan of action*. The bigger *benefit* of this practice is that your actions will be driven from **within** rather from *'with-out.'* They will be fueled with *inspiration* and *energy*. If we were to examine the difference between those who set a *goal* as a *technical* sentence, written on a paper, and those who live its *accomplishment* as a *reality*, we will notice that, when they come to executing their plans, the first group will use words like *"I have to do this"*, *"I must learn that"*, *"I need to finish this"*, while the other group, will use terms like *"I can't wait to do this"*, *"I like learning this subject"*, or *"I am excited to take this step."* Do you see the difference?

The first group treat its tasks and actions as an *outside imposed duty* and a *stressful* factor. It treats them as if they were *forced* upon them, and needs to do it *reluctantly*, so it's coming from a *source of lack*.

For the members of the second approach holding group, on the other hand, we will notice that they are *embracing* their tasks. Their actions are coming from a source of *abundance,* and they are *emotionally* involved in their execution because they are *generated* from the *within* of their *being*.

Changing your terminology will change your perspective, and always remember, *your subconscious is always listening and absorbing!*

We will go further deep in these aspects as we move forward, but it's imperative to already be introduced to them at this stage.

Now we rush to devising our plan in a *methodical* way. As we discussed, the first step should be an *evaluation process*. The purpose of this process is to identify our strengths and weaknesses (in the context of the goal), and to identify the order of the actions needed. This process will expose us to "gaps" in our abilities to carry out the plan of action, and we need to give solutions to filling up those gaps. ***The wider and deeper the gap, the more resources in time, money and energy will be needed*** to *bridge* it. So, take this in careful consideration, and *adjust* your plan, so it can flow. Since the *execution* of the plan will surely *encounter* many *obstacles* and hick-ups along the way *(this is a normal thing and doesn't need to cause alarm)*. It would be *wise* to *minimize* the surprises by *identifying* the *risks* along the way, and giving them suitable *answers* in the *planning* stage.

Once again, I need to stress this. This process carries in it both opportunities and risks. *Refrain from falling in the traps*, don't let the *gaps* **overwhelm** you, and don't submit to *despair*. Nothing is **impossible** and nothing is **unachievable** *(remember that in your mind you have already achieved your goal)*. Focus your thoughts, put doubts aside, and treat the situation without involving any emotions or *fears*, because at this point it is just another *equation*. From here, follow the **Methodology** in the previous chapter and formulate your steps.

Now that you have the *roadmap*, you start taking *action* with *no delay*. Your *subconscious mind* will try to convince you that it's *useless* or that you will *fail* or even that it would be a good idea to *postpone* the execution till a much more suitable time. Those are *normal resistances* that you need to be aware of, and prepared for. Your *subconscious mind* doesn't want to suffer or to work hard or to use too much energy. It wants you to stay safe *(survival is its primary function)* and to stay in your **comfort zone**. The best way to beat this is to take an *immediate action*, if your little voice is saying 'do it *tomorrow*', you *do it today*. If it says *'it is too hard'*, you *try anyway* – **there is no way around this**. It's either to submit to your *comfort zone,* which is basically your **trap zone**, and achieve nothing, or to *break* its boundaries and achieve your *dream. The best time is now*, not in the past and not in the future. As we will discuss in the upcoming chapters, there is *just one real time,* and that is the **present**, all others are *illusions*.

Once you start taking actions, **expect failure and hardship**, it is not a walk in the park. You will need to *gather* your *mental* and *inner strength*s and **not give up**. That is why the process of setting a **suitable goal** for you is so important and even more, the need of you to *believe* in it as a **done reality**. The fact is, that those principles are acting as your *resilience and perseverance soldiers*, pushing away the threats of giving up along the way.

If you fail along the way and *fall* on your face, its ok, nothing happened, *stand up* fast, dust yourself and beware of what you stumbled on and fell, so you *don't fall again*. **Failure is never a reality till you give up** – this is a fact. As long as you are in the race and kicking, you are not a failure.

It is normal and most possible that you will come to a *conclusion* that a *path* you have chosen in your *plan* is not good for you. By all means, *analyse* your options in *light of your goal* and *re-evaluate* your current position. If you find a *better path* to arrive to your *goal*, then take it. **As long as you don't give up on your goal, you didn't fail.** *Adjusting* course in the face of a storm is demonstrating a level of *flexibility in thought and in action, as well as sharp awareness,* which is a higher indication of your *commitment* and *belief*. It stands in the very *contrary* of *failure*. If you find yourself wondering why to keep on trying, remind yourself of the bigger "***Why***" that made you start your *journey* in the first place. Let that *"Why"* *empower* you again and again, each time you doubt yourself or feel tempted to submit to failure.

I hope that giving more depths and context to the previously discussed principles in early chapters, had given you more value and answered some of possible doubts you had. In the next chapters, we will be diving more deeply in the principals of the *inner self* and the *force from within*.

As promised, I will wrap up this chapter with an example of the process of formulating a *goal* and a *plan of action*

Example Plan:

My Higher Goal (vision)

I live a wealthy life, and I am financially free. I am able to provide a comfortable life and future for my family and loved ones.

My Mid-Term Goal (in order to achieve my vision)

I have multiple sources of income in the form of passive income, from various businesses. I use my time to do the things that I love and not the things that I have to.

Example – passive income #1:

Affiliate Marketing Business

Timeframe – one month

Main Activities and Requirements Needed

1. Learning the Domain of Affiliate Marketing (Core).
2. Building a Substantial List of Leads (Core).
3. Setting up My Website, Auto-responders and Tracking Tools (Technical).
4. Writing Emails and Newsletters (Creative).
5. Register to Affiliate Marketing Platforms (Relationships and Community)
6. Find Offers to Promote (Core).
7. Marketing My Offers (Marketing).
8. Startup Budget (Financial).

Evaluation:

Category / Activity	Knowledge		
	Good	Some	Non
Learning The Domain Of Affiliate Marketing			✓
Building A Substantial List Of Leads			✓
Setting Up My Website, Autoresponders And Tracking Tools		✓	
Writing Emails And Newsletters		✓	
Register To Affiliate Marketing Platforms		✓	
Find offers to promote			✓
Marketing My Offers		✓	
Startup Budget		✓	

1. **Conclusion:**

    1. Take a course and develop skills in affiliate marketing.
    2. Learning the principals of gathering leads, and how to maintain them.
    3. Practicing in writing promotional E-mails. Find tools to help me improve in copywriting.
    4. Apply for registration on various leading platforms.
    5. Learn how to identify and choose good offers to promote.
    6. Marketing strategies and platforms that can boost my exposure.
    7. Allocating budget according to priority, expanding the budget as the sales expand.

    ### Diagram – Process Flow

    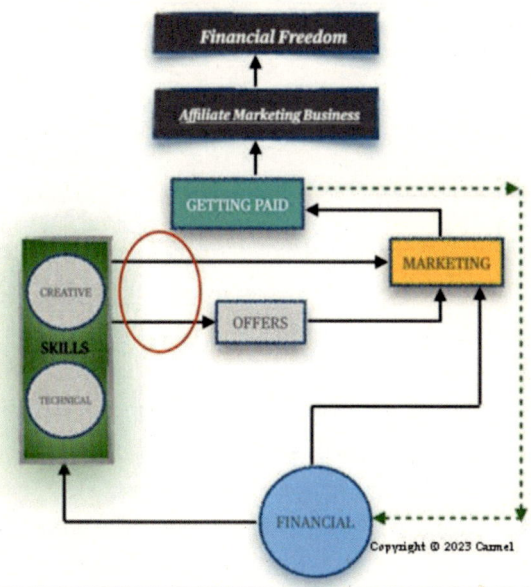

2. **Diagram – Time Table**

Activity	W1	W2	W3	W4	W5	
Learning The Domain Of Affiliate Marketing	▉		Test		Running	Operational
Start Building My List Of Leads			Test		Running	Operational
Setting Up My Website, Autoresponders And Tracking Tools	▉	▉			Running	Operational
Writing Emails And Newsletters			Run		Running	Operational
Register To Affiliate Marketing Platforms	▉				Running	Operational
Find offers to promote					Running	Operational
Marketing My Offers					Running	Operational

"A" - Test -Running The Business

"B" - The Business Is Up And Running

In the example above, I have set my *goal* to establish an *Affiliate Marketing Business* in one **month from now**.

During the *evaluation* process, I understood that I need to <u>undertake a massive training</u> in the subject and to purchase a course, that can give me extensive *knowledge* and *skills* in all the categories that I evaluated as *low/none* knowledge, such as marketing strategies, building lists of leads and etc.

I understand that, depending on my *current knowledge,* I know how to deal with the technical areas. Although, I need a

36

focused training in regards of the specifics of the relevant platforms *(such as designated platforms that are needed to run the business)*.

My start up budget is *sufficient* to get me *started* running my business, but I need to *generate sales* in order to *grow*, since the budget is limited *(evaluated as 'some')*.

The **diagrams** helped me put in a *graphic* way, the paths to *my success*, but also *highlighted* the fact that **acquiring the skills indeed is the critical point** in my plan, and that I need to invest time, energy and money in getting skilled, in order to mobilize my plan.

In the *time table diagram*, I saw that I could *start running my business* once I *passed point "B"*, *after gaining basic skills*, and run some *marketing effort*. I identified my *pivot tasks* as being the *technical and marketing*. Once, I set up the platform and run the *marketing campaign*, I will start running my business **while learning and acquiring more skills.** Of course, all these activities *are not a "one-time effort"*. I will invest the time in keeping *developing my skills* and gain more *knowledge*, keep on building my *list of leads, finding offers,* and constantly improving my skills in writing emails and *marketing*.

However, the business will be *ready to "test run" in week #3*. While I'm still learning, I will start operating my business, gathering information and improving performance, and in week #5 *the business will be fully operational.*

After *stabilizing* the business, basically my work will be to write some E-mails an hour or less a day, *optimizing* my systems and checking that they run smoothly, and occasionally look for *new offers*. From that point on, the business is running on *Auto-Pilot* producing money – *with no connection to my physical location, since I can run it from anywhere on the globe* – **Passive Income!**

Chapter Five
The Mindset

Like any other programme, you will need to *embed* your *plan* in your life. If the plan stays as an external factor, it will never be a part of your life, and it will not be fulfilled.

The *successful* result of our journey is a *combination* between having a *plan* towards a goal, and having the right *mindset* that aligns with those plans and goals. The two parts in the equation are necessary for success. One needs the other in order to achieve success. A plan alone, with no support or resilience, will be doomed to failure, and a mindset alone with no action or destination *(why, what or how)* will stay an abstract and wishful thinking. Our *"Why"* is the ultimate *motivator* and the main *link between both parts,* since they both are *originated* from it.

In order to successfully embed a programme, you need a *software* that is *compatible* and supporting of that *programme*. Otherwise, it would be *rejected* or, in best cases, would operate poorly and with numerous lacks.

Yes, I want you to treat your mind as the most sophisticated computer ever built – because it is. Our mind can process millions of operations in one nanosecond, support and take care of unlimited functions at the same time, without us even thinking about it, and most importantly, it can (and does) create *something* out of *nothing (a thought for example)-* what other computers are not able to!

I know that you have heard a lot about the importance of the mindset and about the concept of its crucial influence on our lives. You may even be one of the lucky ones, that has the ability and skill to plasticize his mindset, and this is awesome. But, if you are one of the many that this term is confusing to them or, *rightfully*, the wide use of it made you doubt it, let me try guiding you through the elusive concept of the inner resilience. Don't worry, I am not going to 'blast' you with fancy terminology or scientific quotes, even though, all that I'm about to talk about, is scientifically researched and proven.

So, what is the Mindset?

Mindset is a certain *mental* state, a complex of *beliefs*, *opinions* and *behaviours* that one is operating *within* it. Our mindset is driven and constructed from our beliefs, the way we see things in life and the way we accept or reject certain ideas or realities. It is a fact, which is not disputed, that our mindset determines the way we approach things in life, our feelings and our relationships with ourselves and with others around us. Our point of view about life and situations we pass through, is mostly driven from this structure, which we call the *mindset*. If you like, look at it as the *software* that is controlling the function of our programme, and determines the results of it. This *software* is called a *Paradigm*.

Researches show that our *Paradigm is* basically formed since the day we are born. Firstly, by our D.N.A, and secondly, by the fact, that a child, till the age of seven, has no conscious ability *(his prefrontal cortex is not yet developed, and therefore it does not filter anything),* his subconscious is wide open and receives all the environmental and behavioural encounters, indexes and stores them. The repetition of these influences form a pattern of thinking and belief, that once the child starts consciously looking at the world around him, the stored information become the reference of his conception of the world. It is also known, that this *software* programming is constantly in progress and updating depending on the person's experiences, relationships, interactions and self-discoveries, till the age of eighteen to twenty-one years old. If a child is born to a poor family, sees his parents grinding each day and still have no real rich life, and he hears his parents complain all the time about how hard life is, or, how hard it is to earn money, or that *"money does not grow on trees"*, then this is the set of beliefs and conceptions that will accompany him throughout all his life. This becomes his *Paradigm,* that is *unconsciously* directing him to choose the choices he chooses, to think the thoughts he thinks and, ultimately, to have the same *results* over and over again.

Once the *Paradigm* is set and goes on **Auto Pilot,** it starts dictating our actions and reactions, ambitions and, ultimately, the belief in our own selves. If we are not aware of our programming, our beliefs and habits, we will always lead a life of frustration, driven from the gap between our *conscious intentions* and our *physical results*.

If we fail to be aware of our *Paradigm*, and we keep on trying the same things over and over again, we will keep on getting the same results over and over again. This missing link in our observation and self-understanding is the most crucial, if we were to change our current reality.

In the beginning of this chapter, I mentioned that, *"In order to successfully embed a programme, you need a software that is compatible and supporting of that programme."* Hopefully, now, this statement is much clearer to you. If our goal and plan of action *(hence the programme)* is not supported by our paradigm *(hence the software)* poor results, if any, will be achieved!

In his teachings, **Bob Proctor**, is describing this unbreakable relationship between the physical result and the mental inner process, in a very interesting and understandable way. The mind has two parts: *conscious and subconscious.* The conscious mind is analysing the reality, it sets goals, it imagines and it thinks. Once the thought or observation is going to the lower layer of our mind, the subconscious, it is *evaluated against* our paradigm, against our beliefs. If it doesn't resonate with them, it will be rejected. The rejection is taking place in forming an *argument* for why we should not do this, based on our beliefs or past experiences. The subconscious' main function is *'survival'* and *'energy saving.'* Once a new idea arises, that would need to consume more energy than the *Auto Pilot* mode does, or that is *risky* in anyway, the subconscious will make sure we don't pursue it or we do it half-hearted and then, along the way, the moment we encounter a *failure* or a *setback* in our results, the subconscious will use this as a *proof* of its argument, that we should not pursue this thought any more, and therefore, we should give up.

Below the mind stands the *body* which is basically our medium to the physical world. The moment the subconscious mind approves and gives the *'go',* an inner process is generated within us, and from there we export it outside. **Bob Proctor** continues to explain that a successful process with successful results needs to come from **UP – DOWN** – *conscious mind to the unconscious mind,* and **INSIDE – OUTSIDE** – *from our inner selves to the world around us.*

A real process, goal or ambition *cannot be generated* from the *outside* world and cannot ignore the programming of our beings. If you would set a goal to be a successful football player, because you see that those players are famous, have money and etc., and you want to imitate them, but you don't like sports activities by nature, then your goal will *never be achieved,* since it doesn't *resonate* with whom *you are.* Unfortunately, a lot of people are *attempting* to follow a goal or carry out a plan that is based from *an outside influence,* and not from an *inside drive.* This, here, is the main bedrock reason for their giving up and failing, and for the difference between those who succeed and excel and those who fail.

One may ask, *how do we know what our paradigm is? How can we identify the programming of our mind?* Well, here is the holy grail question. The key to the inception of success. It is not an easy job nor is it an easy task to know and define *who we are.* I know it sounds strange, saying that we don't know ourselves, but it is a fact that a lot of us don't know who they are. Many times, you can hear people saying things like *"I never thought I had it in me",* or *"this situation showed me who I really was",* and etc. *Extreme* situations and experiences can bring out our *hidden codes* in much more *emphasised* and *externalized* manner.

However, we don't need to wait for these extreme situations in order to know ourselves. We need to develop a *skill* of *observation* and *evaluation* of our thoughts, actions and reactions towards a certain *value* we are pursuing. We need a **deeper awareness** to recognise behaviours and attitudes. It is not necessarily a complicated thing to do, but, it sure, requires deep self-awareness and *open-minded attitude.*

Each one of us has his own *values,* and when I am talking about values, I'm not referring to the moral sort of beliefs. I am talking about the things that we truly hold in high level of importance in our lives, and that we are willing to invest in them the ultimate resources that we all have: **Time, Money and**

Energy. It is proven that, most of these resources are exhausted in a *hierarchy* way from up – down. Meaning that, the most ranked *values* we have will enjoy the most *amount* of these *resources,* and the one after will have less, and so on. It is also proven that most people *exhaust* their *resources* in the first top *five values* they hold important in their lives. After that, whatever *value* or *task* that is coming, it is being easily *given up upon,* and not given any resources, since basically, we don't have what to give any more. To those **downgraded values** attention can be given, just if we were to achieve them or have them with *no effort,* or the need to experience *pain* in achieving them. Basically, we are not willing to endure *pain* in achieving them, but we would like to have their **benefits** with no effort at all. *(Based on the theory of the "hierarchy of values" of Dr John Demartini).*

For example, if a person would like to lose weight, and he actively took action towards his goal – he enrolled in a diet programme, and he joined a gym, but his values and allocation hierarchy of resources do not align with his new goal, he will find himself *quitting* after two weeks. The process will cause him *pain* that he is not ready to have. He wants to lose weight without the *pain* part, and without having to *prioritize* his new goal with other high-level *values* he has. That's why, by the way, we find today that the industry of pills for losing weight is fluorescing. People don't want to have the *pain* in the process or to allocate Time and Energy for it. They think taking a pill will deliver them the *benefit* they *desire,* with no extra *pain.*

The *opposite* example would be a person who sets his goal to have a successful business and to be rich. If this goal is *resonated* with his own *values* and *paradigm,* this person will invest every waken minute and ounce of energy in his business.

His mind will be *receptive* to new ideas and *opportunities* that can help his business, and most importantly, he is *willing* and ready to take the *pain* of *failure* and working hard, since for him, this *is a part of the package*. Not just the collecting of profits, but also the prices he has to pay on his way there.

Those two ideas of *Paradigm* and *Values* are *completing* each other and are working together. One cannot oppose the other, and still have the ability to achieve desired results.

Once we have understood these processes, and how we behave and act in them, what are the things that we are *willing to suffer* for, and what are our *opinions* and *thoughts* on things – then it is obvious that with deep *awareness*, *observation* and *open mind* that we can discover our true selves, in the sense of *Paradigm* and *Values*.

Another way to have insights for our evaluation process, is to get some help from the people that know us the best, like *parents* or *spouse*. People, who you know, they mean you well and are interested in your success. Those close people can *shed a light* on your questions from an *external* point of view of how the others see you. It is a most important point of view, since sometimes, things are so *hidden deep within us* that we fail to see them without an *external* and *objective* point of view. We will go deeper in this idea of having an *external* partner that helps us in *focusing*, *evaluating* and *polishing up* our ideas.

In the next chapters, we will explore the techniques to changing our paradigm and values, so they can be aligned with our goals and plans. But the most important step of these techniques is our *ability* to define what we want to **change**, and this is possible just with the *evolution process* of our *paradigm* and *values*.

Chapter Six
The Power of a Thought

Napoleon Hill, the author of *Think and Grow Rich*, a book that impacted millions around the world and for the first time, placed down a written formula for success *(highly recommended),* says in his book: *"What the mind can believe and conceive, the mind can achieve."* That is to say that, whatever we can think of and imagine, we can create. The condition for this to take place lies in the understanding, that the conception of the mind, is a conscious act that needs to be supported, and formulated by awareness, and subconscious drives, in order for it to take a physical shape.

The power of an idea or a thought, either driven by a *vision*, or by pure *awareness* or *necessity,* has and still impacting our civilization and lives each day. Everything we see around us, or use in our daily lives has started from an idea that someone had, deeply believed in, persuaded, and didn't give up in making it come physical.

An idea that we have that deeply planted in our conscious and subconscious mind, is one of the *strongest forces* that move our world. People have ideas all the time, they have thoughts and they have inspirations. The main difference between a thought that can be transformed into a *physical form* and that which stays *'just an idea',* is rooted in our **belief** and **convection** of it. If we play around with an idea and we don't believe in its possibility to be accomplished, if we can't export it to our subconscious mind, and implant it there as a part of our being, it will not become a reality. We need to *believe* that our idea is *possible* and that we are *capable*.

In the previous chapter, we talked about the subconscious mind and its impact on our results. The subconscious mind has very *unique characteristics* that are standing in *conflict* with our *rational* and *conscious* way of thinking. One of those, is the fact that the subconscious mind has no ability to determine *reality from fiction*, it doesn't know the difference between *imagination and existence*, while, our commonly way of thinking is always considering those differences. This leads to the conclusion that whatever idea or thought we succeed to plant in our subconscious has a place, and is taken in consideration in its existence point of view. The more we contemplate with the idea, and see it formalizing into the physical reality, the stronger it will be embedded in our mind and sought out to be *materialized*. This notion is true and valid for both good and bad thoughts.

If you have any doubts, let's consider something that look very *natural* and *normal* for us to have today, but were not so, before someone had *an idea*.

It was most likely that tonight, you will light up your candle and go on to lightening up all the lanterns in your house, while the city worker will go and pass each street lantern and light them for hours. Fortunately, you don't have to do this. And the reason you don't need, is one man who had an *idea*. It was both *vision* and *awareness driven* idea that changed the world, and how people knew it then, and made our lives today much easier. **Thomas Edison** did not have an easy idea. It was even an impossible and unthinkable one. But he had the conviction of the ability of its existence. *Thomas Edison* did not succeed in inventing the light bulb in one time, actually it took him 2,774 attempts to finally reaching a working design of the light bulb. But he *believed* he could do it, and he didn't *give up* on trying. When he was asked how a great inventor like him failed so many times, he replied, *"I didn't fail, I just discovered 2,774 ways how NOT to do it."* He didn't submit his belief to the failures along the way, he kept his *faith* in his ability to *succeed* and in the ability of the idea to *exist*.

Another example is the invention of the car. If it wasn't for **Henry Ford** having an idea, we most likely would still be using horses as a mean of transportation today. *Ford*, who had no formal high education, was **aware** of the advancement in engineering and technology at his time, which led him to an *idea* of combining those new technologies *(like the steam engine),* and invent a mean of transportation that has replaced the horses and changed the world forever. It was *not an easy or conventional idea,* he was ridiculed and criticized along the way, but he did not *submit* to the *empty noises around him*, and *persisted* on inventing of the first car, till he succeeded, and became the most influencing business man in the world at his time.

I can go on, and on mentioning examples of *ideas* that came to life and changed the world. **The wright Brothers** with the invention of the airplane, **President J.F. Kennedy** who instructed the N.A.S.A. space programme to land a man on the moon, **Steve Jobs** who visioned a computer in every person's palm, and so on examples that our history is full of.

What is important, is the *common link* between all these examples. People who had an idea or a thought, originated in a vision or a necessity, and that they believed in so deeply, and persuaded in *perseverance* and *enthusiasm* till they achieved it and made it *manifest* in the physical world. Those people, by all means, were *extraordinary*. They are extraordinary not because they belong to another human race or that came from outer space, their uniqueness and exceptionality is through their unshakable **belief** and their **conviction** in their ideas to be able to become physical.

You see, the power of an idea or a thought planted deep inside our conscious and subconscious mind, haunts us and makes us *obsessed* with it. This is one of the few cases where the *obsession* becomes a *positive* thing. Unfortunately, usually we tend to embrace the *restraining*, *discouraging* and sometimes *negative ideas* and *thoughts,* rather than pursuing the *visionary*, somehow *revolutionary* and the *demanding* ideas and thoughts. It's the nature of man, – and that's why ninety-seven per cent of the people living a *standard* life while three per cent live an *extraordinary* life.

In my observation, the reason for this is quite simple. The empowering ideas hold an element of *risk, failure, hard work,* 'thinking *out of the box',* and sometimes even against the common beliefs till the point of ridicule. As we already discussed, since the subconscious mind is set to protect us and save energy, these ideas are considered as a *threat*, and thus, *rejected* and driven away under that mask of *fear*, *self-doubt* and *procrastination* to keep and restrain us to our *comfort zone* and safety haven. But the truth is that, no extraordinary achievements can be obtained without taking risks and challenging our *comfort zone!*

This concept, is true for positive thinking as much as for negative thinking. The mind doesn't care what the nature of the thought is. The only confrontation is with our set of beliefs and mindset. But the truth is, that it's always easier for the mind to accept bad thoughts and discouraging way of thinking since it's keeping us restrained to our known and familiar reality. You don't need to invent a new invention to be *extraordinary*. It is way enough and much worthy, if you can hold an idea of *prosperity* for you and your family or community, *believe* in your idea and never give up on it until you *manifest* it into reality. **That is extraordinary!**

Thoughts are mostly *triggered* and *motivated* by an *external* stimulation. But also, they can be driven from an *inner* generator fuelled by the obsession of concentrating on one reality or more. These realities can be valid and actual, but they also can be imaginary and speculated.

Feelings for example, are the perfect *case study* for the above. Fact is, there is no such thing as feelings. There are **emotions** that come within the source of our humanity, and they involve bodily reactions, like when your heart races because you feel excited. They also involve expressive movements, including facial expressions and sounds. It is common among expert to agree that humans have *twenty-seven types of emotions*, such as: *Love, Envy, Compassion, Passion, Surprise, Fear* and *Disgust* and so on. A *feeling,* on the other hand, is not an emotion. It is a *chemical* and a **vibrational** reaction to a *thought* we have. If we were to think about a good memory, a fulfilling feeling would emerge in us, and a smile would appear on our face. On the other hand, if we were to think of a sad memory or a disturbing situation, sadness would fill us, and we will be sad. The *energy* of the *thought* determines the *quality* of our *feeling* and *defines* it, and in return, our body, the medium to the physical world, will project this *"feeling"* we have to our surroundings. We can, with no doubt, change our feelings by changing our thoughts or, as I said before, **changing our perspective in order to change our reality!**

On the contrary of what you may think, this is a very easy

thing to do. The thought has a *life capacity*, it is our *choice,* when to extend its life and when to extinguish it. Disturbing a thought with an *intentional* bringing of other thoughts that we consciously impose in our mind, will cause the passing of the first thought and make room for the newly imposed one. The mind cannot *concentrate* on more than **one** thought at a time, this is a proven fact. When a disturbing and unwanted thought is invading your mind, simply think of another thought to make the disturbing one disappear. It can be taking deep breathes in and out and *concentrating* on your breathing, it can be a joyful or empowering thought or any other technique you find suitable for you.

The important thing is to be **aware** of your *state of mind*, *acknowledge* your feeling and let it pass away without giving it any *interpretations* or *importance*. This is true also for **fears**, since, usually, a fear is a result of a *thought,* that is, if you are not currently attacked by a lion.

You can't control **what** thoughts are coming to your mind. Thoughts come and go. A human mind is able of processing thousands of thoughts in a minute. The *stimulation* of the thought, as we said, is coming from outside sources or inside dynamics. As I see it, the origin of the thought is not important. What is important is to be **aware** of its impact on your state of mind and to recognise if it's **empowering** or **discouraging**, and then act upon it. You can't control what thoughts come to your mind, but you can *control* what to do with them, the **choice** is yours!

When we talk about positive thinking, people tend to ask me, *"Do I need to think passively all the time? It is not possible."* My answer is simple, since you can't control what thought are pumping in your head, it is obvious, there is a chance you will be visited by *negative thoughts*. We are not living in a bubble, and the life around us is happening. So, don't stress if you have a negative thought, this is not important. What is important, is to *identify, acknowledge* and *release*. Choose to *cut* the negative thought out of your mind and replace it with an empowering one, so you can *refuel* your ambitions and inner drive.

It is all Awareness and that's all there is to it!

Chapter Seven
The Impact of the Word

A spoken word is like an arrow shot from a bow. Once it's released, it can't be un-released. If the arrow was shot after a careful aiming and in a deliberate manner, it will hit its target and accomplish the purpose of its release. But, if it's released aimlessly or not in deliberation for a purpose, then it might bring unwanted results and cause unintended damage.

The same goes for the spoken word, or even the unspoken if it's repeating in our heads. When you release a word out of your mouth, there should be an *intention* for its release. A bad word, spoken or written, will offend the listener and cause negative interaction dynamics. And in the majority of cases, once it hits its target, the damage cannot be repaired. The **impact** will always leave a **scar**.

Often, we hear, *"think before you speak"*, *"weigh down your words before you cast them"*, *"keep your thoughts to yourself"*, and other warning suggestions for using our words. This is neither accidental nor philosophical. It is **physics**. A word is an **action** that will have a **reaction**. If we don't consider the reaction, whether it's wanted or unwanted, then we are just blasting words into space with no thought or direction. If we cannot anticipate the chain reaction caused by our words, then we are condemning ourselves to a cycle of *negativity* and *redundant* stress.

When we talk, not just the external environment hears what we say. We *hear ourselves* as well. We seldom consider this, but the impact of a negative word on us is no less than on the environment. I dare say, it is even greater. Our subconscious mind is absorbing, learning, and practicing. As we saw, the subconscious mind has no filters for accepting the information. The subconscious mind does not understand that we were *angry, joking,* or didn't mean what we said. For it, it was heard with our own voice and tone, and was directed instantly to the *"database center"* for processing. What makes the impact of our own words on us even bigger is the fact that our words are accompanied by a *vibrational* quality. These *vibrational* characteristics are different from one emotion to another, and they determine how the mind is perceiving and using the input information.

It gets even more sensitive and distractive if you are talking to *yourself* about *yourself (either out loud or in your own mind)*. We all have those moments of **"self-talk"**. The usual and common form in which we will refer to ourselves is **"I AM"**. This the most powerful statement that can be made, even though we use it thousands of times during the day. **"I AM"** touches your every bit of *being*. It **defines** you. **"I AM"** holds the essence of your being and existence. It is who *you are* that is being described *after*. And whatever description you put after it, it becomes a **directive** that is **embedded** in your *paradigm code*. If you are *not aware,* you will be giving destructive instructions to your mind that, like an arrow shot from the bow, cannot be safely retreated to its quiver.

When someone says, *"I am such an idiot", "I am a failure", "I am not able,"* and so on negative statements. It doesn't matter if he intended or didn't intend to imply that he is really *"a failure"*. The statement after **"I AM"** is an **affirmation**. The subconscious mind will take it exactly as it is, process it, and store it for future use. And when the time comes for that person to start something new, the subconscious will pull that statement out of the archive and remind him that he is a failure, cannot succeed in what he wants to do, and better quit before getting hurt.

The same is true for positive talk. If you empower yourself with a positive **"I AM"**, the process will essentially be the same, but the results will be far more positive on you.

One of the things I find *empowering* and helpful is **Positive Affirmations**. Those can be spoken (or recorded) by you or by someone else. They all start with **"I AM"** or **"YOU ARE"**. The power of *positive affirmations* lies in their **repetition**. Even if in the *beginning* you *don't believe* what you say, it doesn't matter! Once you start repeating the process every day *(even several times a day)* and positively affirming it to yourself, the *rejections* from your mind will get weaker and weaker, till eventually they disappear and the mind accepts the *spoken words* it hears as *facts* to be considered and lived upon.

Everything in life is ***Energy***. ***Life itself is Energy***. Being so, our reality is built out of the ***frequencies*** of different kinds of Energies around us. ***"Everything is Energy and that's all there is to it. Match the frequency of the reality you want and you cannot help but get that reality. It can be no other way. This is not philosophy. This is physics."*** *(Albert Einstein)*. Everything in life, including **words** whether spoken, written, or as thoughts, has Energy, and **Energy** generates **Vibrations**. The *Vibrations* generated by each Energy are ***unique,*** and it affect their environment differently. Pay attention to the *Vibration* in your voice when you talk. It is changing depending on the *Energy of the context*. If you are in a positive and empowering context, then the words and sounds have uplifting and encouraging *Vibrations* that affect your subconscious and your mood, causing you to

Feel Good. While a negative context, like anger, envy, complaining, etc., has a different level of *Vibrations* in the tones and sounds of the words, it's affecting on your subconscious and feelings negatively. Good Vibrations *(hence the expression "good vibes")*, Attract good *Vibrations* from your environment and the **Universe**, and contribute to your ***mindset*** and ability to ***manifest*** your desires, and as ***Einstein*** put it ***"This is not philosophy. This is physics."***

The ***manner*** in which the words are constructed in the sentence has an impact as well. It is possible to say the same thing in two different ways without subtracting the intention. One way can be *damaging*, while the other can be *empowering*. For example, when talking about your activities that serve your goal, don't say, *"I have to", "I must to", and "I am supposed to"*. Instead, say, *"I like to", "I want to", and "I can't wait to..."* One is discouraging and presents challenges of ***rejection***, while the other is empowering and presents a ***drive*** of a ***choice***.

Treat yourself kindly. Don't *judge* yourself harshly for mistakes, failures, or misgivings. *Empower* yourself with positive words and construct your thoughts and spoken verbal expressions with a ***moving-forward*** approach and state of mind. We all fail. Whoever doesn't know failure didn't really try, and who didn't really try didn't take actions on his dreams and ambitions. So instead of beating yourself up for it, *praise* it, be *grateful* for it, and be *fueled* by it. Instead of saying, *"I tried and I failed, it is not for me;"* say, *"I tried and it didn't give the results I was hoping for, but now I have learned a lot and I am grateful for this since, now, I know how to make it better"*, or *"I am grateful for my experience, now I know much more that can help me succeed"*, or *"I know it didn't work well in the past, but now I am learning how to make it succeed."*

Another form of a powerful word is the **Written Word**. The uniqueness of the written word comes from its **creation**. We will need to **combine** our mental and physical skills in the process of creating the written word. The fact that all our senses are involved in the writing of the word, and that it is *physical, actual,* and somewhat *eternal* means that the contribution and impact of the written word cannot be overrated!

In almost all doctrines of psychology and business development, we say, *"Write it down."* Write down how you feel, write down your thoughts, write down your goals and plans, write down your vision and dreams, write it down and place it in front of you. See it as a physical outcome. Read it out loud and hear the words echoing in your mind. When you write something down, you **acknowledge** its **existence** and **approve** its **validity**. You are **aware** of it, and you are **accepting** it. This is a powerful tool that I highly recommend using. It gives you a *perspective* and fills you with *motivation*. Even more, your *awareness* of the words you write and the *intentional* act of writing them, *boosts* the importance of your statements and *implants* your creation deep in your being.

Chapter Eight
Beliefs and Habits

What is the meaning of *'belief'*? What determines if we believe in something or not? How do we "acquire" a belief, if this is possible at all?

Even though the terms *'faith'* and *'belief'* are strongly associated with a *religious* context, it is not a 'religious' act in the common sense of the word. When you ask someone if he believes, and you don't specify in what, he will, usually, automatically assume you are referring to a religious belief. Either you believe in **God** or the **Universe** or in another belief you religiously hold. Most likely, you have never seen, smelled, touched or heard this *Devine entity* you believe in. And yet, the *belief* of its existence is so strong and embedded in your soul and mind, that nobody can dispute *(generally talking)* its existence for you. So, how do you know, if what you believe in, does really exist?

We all, acquire our beliefs from the things we experienced, learned and been told in life. From early ages, most of us, are told that there is a *Devine entity* called **God that** created the Earths and Heavens. Our environment around us – parents, schools, churches and so on, repeatedly taught us this *idea*, till it became so strong in our mind, that for those who believe in **God**, it's an undisputed *fact*, even though, none of them has, actually, ever gotten a *physical proof* of its existence.

In its nature, it is a paradoxical state of mind since, while our *logical* mind has never gotten a physical proof of the existence of **God**, our paradigm and *subconscious* mind **knows** there is a **God**, and therefore, **he is real.** This means that a paradox between the physical dimension, and the way we perceive it, cannot shake down the **foundation** of our **beliefs,** and it will be overcome, without the need of us to even explain it. It is true that sometimes along the way, the *physical dimension* and surrounding's dynamics can, and most certainly will, *challenge* our *belief,* but depending on the *strength* of your belief and the *support* of your *environment* of that belief, you will overcome that challenge and, in most cases, even come out *stronger* in your *belief* than before.

A **Contradiction** between the physical world, meaning the **Results** we have and the **beliefs** we hold, creates a **paradox** or **disharmony**. The effect of this paradox on our decisions and actions is determined by the strength of our beliefs. A *stronger* belief will accept the paradox as **irrelevant,** and keep on going in the same direction despite the difficulties, while, a *weaker* belief will **capitulate** in front of that paradox and, usually, leave us in *"search mode"* for another belief to hang on to. In other words, if your belief is strong enough, the paradox is not important, and should hold no effect on the actions you take in the context of your belief.

*"***Belief (is)** *a mental <u>attitude</u> of acceptance or assent toward a <u>proposition</u> without the full <u>intellectual</u> knowledge required to guarantee its truth (Encyclopedia Britannica)."* The **belief** is **subjective** and it's evolving during time subjectively. It is the knowledge, beyond any *doubt*, that something *exists*. This knowledge allows us to *act* and take *actions* in a certain way, knowing that our actions are *supported* and *included* in a bigger scheme.

We all lead our lives in the way we do, by the beliefs we have. The idea that, belief is *exclusively* reserved for a religious context, is *absurd*. Everything that we do each day of our lives, each action or decision we take, is in its ***core*** connected to a belief we hold. It can be a political context, a financial context, relationship context, or even in how we perceive others, those are all led by the beliefs we have.

We are used to the saying *"seeing is believing"*. This may hold true in some cases, mostly those cases that involve external interactions or interactions with other people, for example: *"I will believe he is really changed, when I see it with my own eyes."* But on the other hand, **no one** who believes in **God** would say, *"When I see God, I will believe he exists"*. When it comes to our *inner* and *spiritual* being, we don't seek a proof for our beliefs, meaning that, when we are considering the ***inner self interactions*** deep in us, we don't need *to see* in order to *believe,* rather, **we believe therefore we will see.** The context is reversed from "*Seeing Is Believing*" to "***Believing Is Seeing***". First you believe in something and then you act upon it and achieve it, or as **Bob Proctor** put it, *"Believe and you shall receive."*

Depending on our stage of life, experiences and results, we can change our beliefs or acquire new beliefs. We already know that the subconscious mind is the 'computer' that holds everything that we are, including our beliefs. We can change the programming in this computer by perseveringly following, and convincing ourselves of a desired reality or outcome. **REPETITION** is the secret in changing or creating our beliefs. The power of **Repetition** is enormous, it *imposes* a desired conception and *implants* new and wanted *pattern* in our subconscious mind. By using the ***methods*** described previously: setting a clear ***goal,*** and treating it as it was already *achieved*, repeatedly using of empowering *affirmations*, using empowering spoken and written *words* and disconnecting unwanted discouraging *thoughts* by creating positive ones, seeking out and learning new *skills* to help us and support our actions, developing a high level of *awareness* in terms of what is happening inside of us *right now,* and the effect of it on us, and in result, being *focused* on the reality that we want to achieve, if all these are done repeatedly and determinedly, we will, in time, with no doubt, create the desired *patterns* we want.

Let's say that you aim to be wealthy. You set up your goals and the plan to achieve them. You start the process of creating the right mindset, and you disconnect yourself from unwanted thoughts. A week has gone by, or a month, or even a year, and nothing has happened to indicate to you that your reality is about to change, or that you are any closer to achieving your goal than when you started. Evermore, negative things are happening in your physical world, and your financials are deteriorating. This will surely affect your resoluteness in the process and might cause you to give up. A strong *belief* in your way and your *goal*, seeing your *desired* life as already been *manifested* in front of you (like would a *devoted* religious person sees himself rewarded in *heaven),* will guide you through the turbulence, and keep you on the *path*. When the *belief* is strong, the *paradox* will be *overcome*.

A very basic *corner stone* of the indication of *belief* is that which is associated with the principle of *trust.* When we believe, we trust. We trust the thing in which we believe, to *deliver* us the subject of its purpose. Some believe that, if they *work very hard*, they will have *money,* some believe that if they have a *university degree*, they will have a *better job*. Each belief holds in it the principal of trust that we will receive that subject of purpose.

Being so, the principle of trust is a very important component in our belief. We do what we believe is right for us, and we trust that we will get the right results. This principle of trust, is one of those that give us the *support* and *resilience* in moving on, despite external immediate results we may have. Doing otherwise, we declare that we don't trust, and if we don't trust, then we don't believe. So, in order to release ourselves from the tension of the paradox, we need to **Let Go**, trust the *process* and *release control*. We cannot always control the results of the process. It is a *dynamic movement* of many *moving parts* that have a life of their own. Furthermore, the ability to *let go,* and trust the process can, and most possibly will, *create* new opportunities and unexpected breakthroughs that were not on the table when we started. Releasing control does not mean to quit being involved, we need to be involved and present, aware and alert, but, at the same time, to release ourselves from the occupation with the momentary result, and put our energy in the need to persist. **Persistence** is the secret of success, and momentary results or attempts to control them will, no doubt, *negatively* affect it.

Our ***Universe*** is vast, and some say it is endless and yet, it is still expanding. This is a proven fact. Our ***mind*** is marvellous in its built and abilities. They are both *Energy* or, at the very least, *conducting* Energy. Our mind is a ***microcosmos*** that holds in it *all* the *abilities* that we require. Some are conscious to us, some are not, some are less active, and some are more active. The *degree* in which an *ability is conceived*, is largely *dependent* and projected by the *inner powers* that drive us in life. Our *Values, Paradigms and Beliefs* stimulate the ***mind*** in seeing or perceiving things in life the way it does. Like the Universe, we can *expand* our mind and create new connections to change the degree of its *consciousness* by working and ***reprogramming*** our subconscious and by expanding our knowledge.

Think of it this way, two persons can have the same last model of iPhone. One is using its basic features, making calls, and maybe, browsing the web, while the other, is using it as a personal assistance that is giving him an edge in his daily life. They both have the same model, that have the same technological ability and functions, but there are having a *different experience* while using it. Our brain is highly advanced. If we don't put the energy and time to expand our **knowledge** and abilities in *utilizing* the mind in our *Goals achieving process*, by constant **learning**, **repetition** of empowering programme, expanding our skills and **beliefs**, we will be just like the first person that uses the iPhone as a 'send'– 'end' calls only.

One of the most ***observable*** and ***detectable*** indicators of our *beliefs* and inner *paradigm,* is our **habits.** Our habits can tell us a lot about ourselves, and what we believe in, and hold high in our value scale. You may think that habits are a force of nature that cannot be changed, this is far from being the situation. Habits are *behavioural manifestation* of our conception on various aspects in our lives. Therefore, they are an *effect* and not a *cause*. Being so, and by careful observation and deep awareness, *examining* our habits can shed a light on our *beliefs* and *values* in life and help us detect those *codes* in our *'programme'* that are not aligned with our desired reality, and need changing.

This is a very important *benefit* that we can have from observing our *habits*. However, the bigger benefit of ***habits'*** awareness is the fact that, changing them in a *constructive*, *aware* and *methodical* manner, and adapting a repetitive pattern of behaviour, will affect our subconscious mind and reprogram it.

Years ago, when I started my journey in self-development, I

needed a high level of energy in order to identify, evaluate, discover and track the things I needed to change, in order to support myself on the path to my goals. I used several methods to create new habits and to make sure I stick to them. So, for example, I used my calendar to plan and make time for the activities I needed to do, like daily mediation session, a designated time for writing or for learning something new and etc. It wasn't easy to do it. My *programmed habits,* that were on "*Auto Pilot*" mode and led me to my *comfort zone* of saving energy and avoiding change, were constantly trying to pull me back. I needed to fight. I decided to myself I will not give up, I *believed* in my way and didn't let hardships, external observations or even remarks from the people around me, to stray me from my path. I was **consciously** allocating and prioritizing resources for my new habits that I wanted to implant. It wasn't long till I started feeling changes inside of me, and I started noticing that my *perspective* of the world is changing, my *focus* shifted to *constructive* thoughts instead of negative *interpretations* and analysis of *past* experiences, doubts and fears about the future. I started to see the effect of all those on my ability to achieve my goals. This change was *noticeable* for the *environment* around me as it was for me.

Connecting to myself, and being *aware* of the moment and its consequence, *positioned* me in a different place from which, the point of view of the world revealed things I have not seen before. I was very *persistent* in my new way, and I was driven by a *belief* that was getting stronger and stronger by the day. Today, I don't need to put any energy in it any more. The new *habits* became the ones that are on *Auto Pilot,* while the old ones disappeared away.

New habits and thoughts are like a new uncharted zone that

you find yourself in. It is hard to find the right direction in the beginning, but after you *familiarise* yourself with the new surrounding and *normalise* the activity as a natural one of your daily routine, it becomes much easier to implant and perfect those new *habits* into your life.

It reminds me of when we go to a new place and see new things. They look amazing to us and exceptional. But, if we were to move and live in that place, all these amazing things will be **normal** to us, and it will be natural to see them. They will still be amazing, and we will still be admiring them, but we will not put *energy* in thinking about them any more since they are a *normal* part of our scenery. The same is the situation with a *new habit.* Maybe, in the beginning, it looks demanding and hard to do, but once we live it, it becomes a **normality,** that without it, something will be missing in our lives.

Identifying, what *destructive* or *limiting* habits and beliefs you have in your life, is a **mindfulness process**. It brings you to a higher level of *intimacy* with yourself. Sometimes we will need help in identifying those patterns in our lives. Since, as we said earlier, there are aspects that are so very deeply hidden inside of us, that we will need an *external* observation or point of view to see them. Here, I recommend that you ask or share your process with someone who is close to you and knows you well. This person needs to be someone that you *trust*, someone you know he has *good intentions* and is *concerned* about your *well-being,* and truly wants your success. It can be a spouse, a parent or a close friend that has a *proven history* of telling you the truth, supports you and has the *courage* and the *goodwill* to *advise* you, even if it's against your comfort. Having someone like this beside you will give you the external point of view you need, and during the process itself, will become a kind of an *"Accountability*

Partner" that pushes you back onto the path, if you were to fall out of it. You need to have an ***open mind*** though, and be ready to accept hearing opinions or a point of view, that you might find uncomfortable.

Our *environment* has a big influence on our ability to change pattern of habits, and eventually to *achieve* our *goals*. The people in our lives, the organisation of our home and workplace, the things we keep close to us and the things we keep far, our diet and health aspects, all have an *impact* on our lives and our *ability* to *accomplish* things. If you surround yourself with friends that have no ambition or that their *values* are not *aligned* with the values you *seek*, then, those people will hold you back and *discourage* you. If your house is not organised, and you don't have the physical place that can support, for example, you're learning process, it will be even harder for you to *breach forward*. *Distance* yourself from any environment that you *recognise* as *not contributing* to your goals, or that is *limiting* your *success*, and adjust and build a new environment that will.

This process needs to be a ***gradual*** one. You need to assess your ability of dealing with changes and make sure you don't ***overwhelm*** yourself by the process. Take it slow, and advance step by step. Start with small changes and develop your ability to *accept* changes. In the same time, find out what is the best way for you to ensure success by adapting a ***methodology*** that is right for you.

Building a mindset needs to be dealt with *care* and *mindfulness* due to the resistances we will encounter, and the chance of *overwhelming* ourselves. At the same time, it needs to be a *resolute* and *unwavering* process since, even the *smallest* yielding and straying from it, will result in graduate *capitulation* and failure. We need to *normalise* our *habits* and our **Goals** to the mind. Whatever is conceived as *normal* to the mind, the mind will have much easier time in *accepting* it. If the mind *believes* that it is *normal for me to be wealthy and rich*, then there is no reason why I shouldn't be, and thus, the *resistances* in accepting the changes and habits to reach that **Goal**, will be significantly *reduced*.

Chapter Nine
Awareness

If you would ask me, what is the one thing I need to take from this book, I would tell you, it is this chapter. In my belief, **Awareness** is the very most important key to success. You can't lead your life without being aware of its direction, and you cannot shift from one side to another if you are not aware of where you stand, or of the significance of your position in the whole scheme.

There are different levels and aspects of awareness. We will try to discuss them all. However, if you paid close attention to the previous discussions, you would have noticed that, the principle of *awareness* is *present and intertwined* in each and every one of them, either by *indication* or by *essence*.

The definition of **Awareness** is the "***knowledge** that something exists, or understanding of a situation or subject at the **present time** based on information or experience*" (Cambridge dictionary).

It is the ability to live the *current moment* and *acknowledge* the *present* environment, *influences* and *opportunities* that are happening to us at the current time. It gives us the ability to become the leaders of our lives, rather than being the passengers in our own lives.

Everything exists in this world, and yet, ***nothing*** exists if you are not ***aware of it***. Our world is whole and complete, nothing is missing, and nothing is in lack. The nature is an abundant entity which knows no *lack*, it knows how to regenerate and balance itself, and provide the existence conditions to all creatures, including the human race. The fact that we don't see this clearly has to do, mainly, with the understanding that ***the mind sees what it wants to see***. Or better to say, the mind sees everything, but concentrates and remembers what is important to us as it sees it, depending on our Programme of beliefs and values.

Two people can look at the same situation and see two entirely different things. Even though, it is all there, the situation at hand is hundred per cent whole and complete, they both see and emphasise different aspects of the whole picture. This is because their minds are *programmed differently,* and their observation is led by different set of *values* and *guidelines*. In result, they *interpret* the reality in front of them differently, and they draw different *conclusions* from it. How many times did you go together with a friend or a spouse in a place, and the things you remember from that experience is entirely different from how the other saw it? Our awareness of the things around us is directly *affected* by the level of *importance that* the mind gives, to the *visual signs* it receives. If we are *'passengers',* then we will not interfere with the process, and we will get whatever is *comfortable* to the mind, and that *aligns* with our *paradigm*. If we are the *'leaders'*, however, we will *consciously* be *present* in the moment, and decide what inputs we would like to have from the experience.

The same exact idea is with our being. We are all born the same. We are given the same *abilities* and *faculties*, the same brain structure and the same body functions *(generally speaking)*, and we all have the same twenty-four hours a day. We are born with *everything* that we need, in order to *live* and *flourish*. This goes for the ability to have *wealth* and to *prosper* as well. We all have the same amounts of *hours* a day, we *breathe* the same air, and we *walk* the same earth. And yet, some of us are *extraordinary successful,* and some are *not*. Why is that?

Even though we are given the same gifts at birth, on the way, our experiences and our beliefs define the use and the utilization of those abilities. They define our perspective of things, and they define our values. Eventually, they define the ***directives*** for our *awareness levels and focus*. It is like the features of that new iPhone. All iPhones come with the same features, but not all users get the same results and benefits out of them.

Awareness and **Mindfulness** are the bedrocks for our decisions and behaviours. The way we understand the things that happen to us **NOW**, has a direct effect on the actions we take **NOW**, which in turn will determine the results of our process to achieving our goals.

Furthermore, **Awareness** and **Mindfulness** don't just have effects on our external manifestations, but also, and perhaps, more importantly, on our inner process, mainly speaking about our ***Intuition.*** We are all born with the ability of *intuition.* It's a ***primal faculty*** that origins in the *intuition of survival*. If a danger is heading our way, we often find our actions to be automatic and intuitive to avoid getting harmed by that danger. Sometimes we can't even explain our action, and how we avoided the danger of being harmed, in a split of a second reaction. *Intuition* is a higher faculty we all possess. Again, some of us have it more trained and sharpened, some less. The level of *awareness* we have around certain things determines the level of *intuition* we might have. The more you are in the moment and aware of it, the more you are focused and aligned with your beliefs, and the more you are in control of your thoughts, the more support for ***intuitive thinking*** you will have. *Intuition* comes from inside; it comes from your subconscious. It doesn't go through any logical analysis before it appears in your head or before you feel it. Just after its appearance, you will have the chance to logically and consciously evaluate it.

Nothing we do in life comes without work and some level of **Risk**. It can be an *immediate* risk or an *accumulating* risk. Everything we do, we need to actually and actively take an action for it. From small things like brushing our teeth till bigger things like building a successful business. The only difference would be in the amount of work *(energy, time, money)* we need to invest, and the level of *risk* we would *accept* on ourselves. The flow of the execution of the actions we take and their success will heavily be *influenced* by a complex of factors that we already discussed, one of which is the **Skill** factor. The more *skilled* we are at executing an operation, the easier and smoother the execution will be. *Skills* are an *acquired ability*. If you put energy into learning and developing a new *skill*, you will have it. As I see it, apart from being a *birth given faculty*, Awareness can be an *acquired skill* as well. Developing our awareness is a possible thing. It's a process that can be controlled and led by a decision to acquire and train ourselves in a new skill.

As we possess a high level of awareness for a process or an action, we will be *alerted* to the risks that that action poses and the skills needed, in order to successfully achieve that process, as well as to the other factors needed to support us on our path. This is a very important thing to understand. This is the *foundation* of our *assessment* in the planning stage, and once the process has started, **Awareness** and **Mindfulness** will be the main aids with which we can, objectively and successfully, assess our position compared to where we want to be. *Awareness* and *Mindfulness* are the main drivers for our decisions and course of action.

The moment we take it upon ourselves to go through a certain process, we **commit**. A *commitment* is a *contract* between our mind and body. Once we sign this contract with the signature of a **decision**, we become *responsible* for our part of that *commitment*. **Accountability** and taking **responsibility** are both very important components of success. Whatever action we take, whatever decision we follow or whatever conduct we choose, it is *ours* to carry. It is our *responsibility,* and we need to take *accountability* for it. You cannot hang your failures or setbacks on an external factor *(if it is not a natural disaster)*. **Nobody** is *forcing* you to take that *specific decision.* They may deceive you into making that decision, but in the end, it is **your** decision to make. And once you make that decision, it is fully your *responsibility,* and you hold *full accountability* for it. This level of *awareness* will help you *adopt* the process, and be *involved* in making it succeed. Once you are aware of your accountability, you have different inner drives in action that are generated from *within* and shaped by your belief in what you are doing.

Awareness is a sign of *focus*. If you are *focused*, then you are *aware* of what is happening in the specific area of activity at the current moment. Focus is crucial in everything we do in our lives, and sometimes it can be the difference between life and death. If a driver does not focus on driving and on the street, his chances of having a life-threatening accident will grow exponentially. You can work and *improve* your focus by *training* your mind to *concentrate* on the *current moment*. This can be achieved through daily **Meditation**. It can be a guided meditation or an open meditation that you lead yourself. In the beginning, at least, I would strongly advise the use *of guided meditation*. It is most helpful and leading. The *purpose* of the *meditation* is to *clear* the mind and sort the thoughts out. When you practice meditation daily, your ability of *focusing* and *concentrating* on the present moment and a specific subject will be enhanced drastically.

Life is not *single-dimensional*. Everything we do exists in a *multidimensional* form and interaction. We cannot separate certain aspects of our lives, and pretend they don't have effects on others. Since we all have *limited* and *finite resources*, everything we do in our multidimensional environment will compete for those resources. The most explosive clashes we might encounter in this sense, for example, are those between business and family. If one is achieved at the expense of the other, it will create an inner struggle and, sometimes, a feeling of guilt that will diminish the accomplishments of the other. A developed awareness will assist you in *detecting* the *imbalances* and help you *rebalance,* or at least explain your point of view or set *expectations* with other people involved in your *multidimensional* reality. **Awareness** and **Mindfulness** are imperative for understanding the need for balance in our lives. They highlight the fact that, in order for our success to *manifest*, we need a *multilayer support system,* and a mental haven, of which the most important of all, but not exclusively, is family. In order for us to manifest success and happiness, each layer in our *Multidimensional* reality, according to its *value* in our being, needs to *nourish* the other!

The last and maybe most important aspect of *awareness* is the **Conception of Time.** The essence of awareness, as we have discussed it till now, is that it exists in direct connection to an acknowledgment of the existence of something **AT THE PRESENT TIME.** I will skip ahead and tell you right now that there is just one time that exists, and it is the **Present** time, the *Right Now* moment. **Past** and **Future** do *not exist,* and any occupation in them is basically *senseless!*

The Past does not exist. It's a memory in our *subjective* minds that is usually *presented* to us depending on the scope and essence of the action in question. So, for example, if we were to fail in a business, the mind *(our subconscious)* would show us the *suffering* from that failure rather than the things we *learned and achieved.* This is a *defensive* action in order to "Protect Us" from more "Pain". Or, if you had been betrayed by a friend, the mind would hold that *negative* idea, and fail to present the other good friends you had or have that were loyal to you and came to your aid when you needed them. Furthermore, our past is our *memory* of *events* that don't exist anymore. ***They are done and gone***. They hold no real effect on our current situation or ambitions. They don't *define* us, nor do they *define* our present. Those past experiences or failures need to be *acknowledged* as *helpless,* and as holding no power over us. We need to develop the **Awareness** needed to be able to look at them in a *constructive* way, and take from them the things we have *learned* and *accomplished*.

So, the ***Past does not exist,*** and thinking about it or giving it power over us goes against any logical thinking.

The Future does not exist either. It's something that hasn't happened yet and holds *no ground* in our lives.

Consider this: one year from now, on the same day and at the same time, it's going to be your ***Present.*** If you are too *consumed* by thinking what is going to be in the ***Future***, then in one year from now, you will still be *in the same place,* worrying about what is going to be in the ***Future***. ***"Worrying about the Future is a down payment on a problem you may never have"*** *(Joyce Meyer).* We are certainly expected to *plan* for the Future and *prepare* it. But not living it now. Remember, when you arrive in the *Future*, it will be your *Present*, and unless you actually took action in your *"Current Present"*, the *"Future Present"* will not be as you planed.

Therefore, the *Future does not exist,* and worrying about it instead of taking action now really makes no sense at all.

The Only Real Time We Have Is the Present!

The *actions* we take now will *determine* our *Future*. We can't wait for the *Future* in order to do things or carry out plans, since the Future will never arrive. The best time to act is always NOW. *Whatever you do now will determine your life tomorrow.*

It doesn't matter if you are not hundred per cent ready or hundred per cent with an action plan. What is really important is to *Take Action, and start Right Now. Motorise* that idea in your head and see it *taking a physical form now.* Otherwise, it will always be an idea somewhere on a *shelf* under the *"in the Future"* label.

A complete *awareness* of the conception of time is crucial. Any other occupation, in the past or in the future, is *utterly senseless. Planning* for the future is not *worrying* about the future. It is obvious that the *accomplishment* of your goal is going to be in the future. Even if this future is one hour from now, it is still the future. Once your plan is ready, take action *Right Away,* and start executing it. Each tree you plant **NOW** is another tree in your plantation of **TOMORROW**.

Practicing Awareness and Mindfulness is the tip of the pyramid, from which all previous components will be affected and touched.

"The Only Limit to Our Realization of Tomorrow Will Be Our Doubts of Today." (Franklin D Roosevelt)

Chapter Ten
Take Charge

I believe *everyone* has all the tools and abilities for success already imprinted in him. We are all born whole and with the same faculties. The key to accessing those abilities lies in the conscious knowledge of their existence and in the **Repeated Practice** to activate them, **Normalise** them, and set them up in *Auto Pilot* mode.

Up until now, we have explored a wide complex of ideas that are proven to contribute to and lead to *success* in general and *financial* success in particular. Those ideas represent the *concept* that we are the **leaders** of our lives. We are the *'drivers'*, not *passengers*. The difference will be rooted in the act of **Choice**. We have the choice to be leaders or followers, drivers or passengers. I know that making a choice is a hard thing, and that's why sometimes people tend to postpone it. In my opinion, this *procrastination* is driven from the place of lack of *awareness*. People who are aware of what is on the scale, and what benefits, and impact a *decision,* will have on their lives tend to make the choice of change pretty fast. This is the importance of the "*Why*" in your journey. If the "*Why*" is clear and big enough, it will motivate you to take action. Of course, it is just up to us whether to make the *choice* or not, to take the *decision* or not, and to take *charge* of our lives or not.

But, if you have *dreams* and you *envision* your life and the lives of your loved ones in a certain way that does not align with the reality you are living, then, my friend, it is that time to **Take Charge**. The road to change is not easy, and we covered the *mental* resistances and *roadblocks* that make it hard. The good news is that once you are *aware* of those obstacles, you have already made half the way through towards the desired change. I would like you to transform yourself from a **Reactionist** into an **Action-Taker**. To stop *reacting* to what is happening **TO** your life, and start *taking actions* to make things happen **IN** your life.

Failure is a part of life. "***Those who don't fail, didn't even try***" *(Denzil Washington)*. Failure is not a failure until you quit. As long as you are trying and pushing, learning and adjusting in light of your **Goal**, you are **Wining!** You might quit a *tactical activity* or a *direction* on your path that you concluded had no *contribution* to your goal; this is good. It means that you are *aware* of the results and contribution of your actions, and that you are maintaining ***flexibility of thought and action***. As long as you don't quit the **Goal,** you didn't fail.

Fears may ***hinder*** you from taking actions. It can be a fear of failing or a fear of losing what you have. It can be the fear of the change itself or the uncertainty of the process you are about to undertake. Whatever your fear is, I want you to understand that, it is just a ***manifestation*** of a ***doubtful thought*** that has no ground in reality. It doesn't matter if your fears are driven by the *past* experiences and failures you had, or the uncertainty of the *future*. The solid fact remains that ***they don't exist right now in this moment***. They are projections of shadows from the past or from doubtful thinking. I am not suggesting that you ignore your fears. Ignoring your fears will just push them into a deeper place in your mind, ready to resurface in the most inconvenient moment, or when you hit a pump on the road. If you have a fear of failing, then the first time something does not go as planned, your fears will re-emerge and hinder you from moving forward, and you will start thinking: *"My fears were true; this will never work."*

You need **NOT** *ignore* your fears. You need to **confront** your fears. *Acknowledging* your fears, and understanding their roots is an important step in *gaining resoluteness* on your journey. When *confronting* your fears, understand that they are there to *protect* you. They are the tool of your *survival subconscious* to avoid *pain* and *suffering* as well as *save energy and resources*. So, don't *overlook* them, and don't be *harsh* on yourself for *having* them. Just *observe* them, don't react to them, and gently **dismiss** them aside. Pass no *judgment* in the process. Just *observe, acknowledge,* and *dismiss*. Use your *"Why"* to assist you in gaining confidence and motivation. Your **Fears** are the *weapon* your *survival subconscious* uses to stop you from taking action, and your *"Why"* is the *shield,* you need to use to defend your *actions*.

Your journey is yours and yours alone. You are the one who decides how your life should look like, and what actions you need to take in order to get there. *Nobody* is living your life instead of you, and *nobody* has the right to tell you how high you should aim. Understanding this and adopting it, is the *essence* of *taking charge* of your life. Don't think about what others may think about you or your beliefs. Don't let those who *criticise* you, because you're *prioritizing* your resources, or having a *Goal* in life that is not according to their expectations, hold you down and prevent you from taking action. As long as you keep an *acceptable balance* that *resonates* with your *values,* you only need to do what you *truly believe in,* and make the *choices* you *believe* are best for you.

At the same time, don't look at others around you and *don't judge* them. They have *their own* journeys in life, and like you, **they see it as they believe it**. If you have someone close to you who you care about, and you think he needs guiding or focusing, first ask for his or her **permission** to do so. *Understand* the *values* that lead them and the *dreams* they hold for themselves before you get involved in their process. **Don't** *'lecture'* them. **Don't** *judge* them or their choices. Just try to help them see things clearer from **their** Goals' and Values' point of view, not yours. Guide them in the *"How"* not the *"Why"*. You are allowed to express your opinions, how you see their choices and actions, and what advises you would give them in that regard, as long as you don't do this in a *judgmental* manner and you **Empower** them instead of **Discouraging** them.

Taking charge means taking **Responsibility**. You embrace **Accountability** for your actions and choices. Any successes or failures you will encounter, are *yours* to *account* for. This is not a *discouraging* fact, but rather a very important and *empowering* one. Think about it for a moment: if you are accountable, that means you are in charge, you are the director of your actions, you made the decisions that brought you to this point in life, and you are the only one who understands the *motives* behind them and the *purpose* they stood for. Being so, you are the only one who can fully understand the meaning of the results you are having, and what needs to be adjusted or changed in order to move forward. You cannot escape the simple fact of life: you have a choice. Your lack of acceptance to assume that role of choice-taking does not give you the right or the legitimacy to **delegate** the consequences of your lack of action to another external factor or person. ***You are not a victim***. *Victimizing* yourself will take the power out of your hands. You will be the *passenger* who has no say in what direction he should proceed, since he doesn't know how he got to this point in the first place. If you *surrender* charge to an *external* environment or party, then you have no *control* over your position since you were *led,* not *leading*.

I see people looking at other people, and saying, *"That guy has everything going for him; me, whatever I do is going against me."* I don't know if it's *funny or sad*. It is *funny* because we don't know what that guy has gone through and what mindset he adopted to attract what he wants. We don't know what *values* he holds dear in his life, and we don't know how many times he *fell* along the way. We actually don't know *anything* about his *journey*. All we see is the **tip of the iceberg** of his success, and we don't take into consideration admiring the hard work, either *mentally* or *physically*, that he put in, in order to arrive where he is now. At the same time, it is *sad*. It's sad because we are getting *exactly* what we want. We just don't know that this is what we are aiming for unconsciously. *If* we are not achieving the results we want and are not manifesting the dreams of our lives, *then* we are missing something in the process. And, since we have no *awareness* of what that thing might be, we'd rather look at others and *pity* ourselves through them. *It is sad!* I find *Envy* to be a most **destructive** quality one can have, a quality that leaves no place for *Love*. Envying others for what they have achieved, and have, is demonstrating both *bad character and weak personality*. Instead of looking at others and envying them, look at *yourself* and understand why you are not getting the results they are getting. Instead of diminishing their success, draw an example and an encouragement out of them: *"if they can do it, then you can too."*

I would like you to approach your life and mange it, as if you were a **CEO** managing a big *company*. *Technically*, our lives are no different than a highly sophisticated multilayer project or organisation. And like any CEO, we have *full charge* over it. We are the ones having the *vision* of our lives, and how it should look like. We are the ones setting the *course* of our lives, setting *goals,* and determining a *method* of *action* to achieve them. And just like a CEO would do, we need to *evaluate* our current position compared to our goals and draw *conclusions* regarding what we should *enhance* in order to get there faster. A CEO would understand the *organisational dynamics* and have a balanced management approach towards his employees, staff, suppliers, and contractors. Not far from the understanding needed for us to *navigate* our *multidimensional environment* and maintain a balanced harmony with it. Also, the same as approaching a business Goal in a company, we need to understand the effect of *Knowledgeable Skills* needed from us to achieve our goals and *acquire* those that we don't have or have insufficiently. Furthermore, we need to *Measure* our *successes* and *failures* in light of the *goals* we are marching towards and adjust course as needed. Like any visionary company that draws *Inspiration* from its competition but *acts originally* according to its *core beliefs and values,* we should act too. We should take *accountability* as well as assume *responsibility* for our results and *achievements, successes* and *failures,* exactly like any other *serious* CEO would do. A successful CEO has a *vision* for his company, and he is willing to take *Calculated Risks* in order for him to be *extraordinary* in his accomplishments, as we *should* do in order for us to lead an *extraordinary life.*

Chapter Eleven
Launch Your Success

In this last chapter, we will examine the ideas brought to you till now in a practical manner in which you can recognise your next steps towards achieving your success and wealth.

But first, I would like you to pay attention to the following illustration: it represents the *wholeness* of the *mindset,* and draws out the *harmonies* needed inside each one of us!

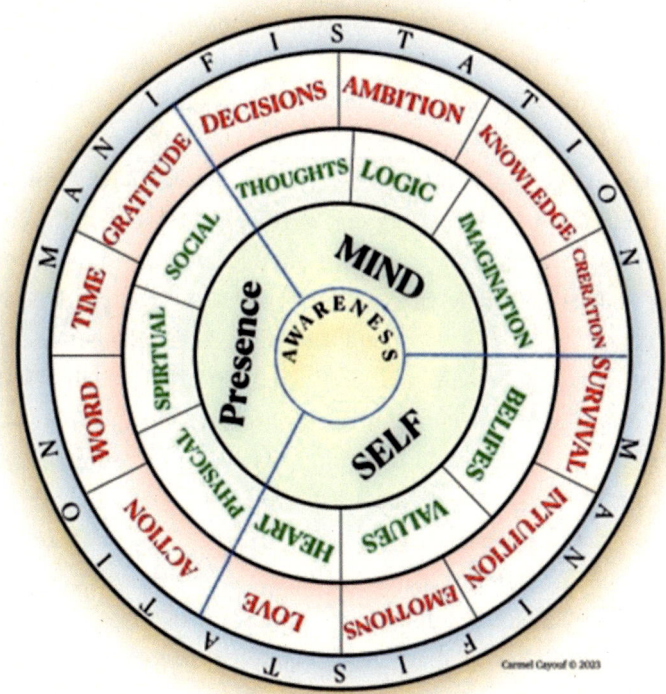

Our ability to manifest and create is highly affected, and even, motivated by the *inner harmony* we achieve. Each quality, either a basic quality, or a secondary one, has its own *'weight'* and *'frequency' (vibration)*. We have to *harmonise* the qualities we have so they will work in *balance* and don't come at the expense of each other. Each quality has its *counterpart*, and by increasing one above the desired and wanted level, you are by nature, decreasing another. Since the circle is *whole,* and it's hundred per cent allocated, it is only logical that if we give one quality more than we should, another one will be lacking and will cause some degree of *suffering*. The balance is *not universal.* It is **subjective** for each of us depending on our personalities and ambitions. Furthermore, a decrease or neglect of one or more of the secondary qualities will have a **chain reaction** that is negatively affecting all the way back to the *core* of our *mindset*, and obviously *vice versa*. It is a *"closed system"* that you cannot escape. However, we can, and should, amplify and grow ourselves as a whole, which in turn will grow the hundred per cent to include more resources for us to allocate. This we can achieve by constant *learning* and *developing*, by enhancing our *awareness*, which is the *core* of it all, and by connecting to our inner selves to understand those places in which we are consuming *negative* energy and transform it into a *positive* one. I know this might sound a bit confusing, but think about it for a moment: if you are consuming resources *(Time, Money and Energy)* for thinking and analysing the *past,* for example, you will not have enough resources left to allocate to your *imagination* and *ambitions*. The resources are a *given parameter* in the system. Using them in unwanted activities will consume them exactly as a wanted activity would, maybe even more. So, you might think you don't have enough resources for certain things you *"would like to do someday"*, when in fact you are **wasting** those resources on *unproductive* things. It is much like understanding the Chinese *Yin and Yang,* the bad and good are competing with one another in the same given space.

The components need to work *harmoniously* in order for our **mindset** to be ***supportive*** of our goals, exactly like the parts of a car would work in a certain *harmony* to support the performances of that specific car. The *harmony* is decided and is *a product* of who you are, exactly like the *harmony* of parts working in a certain car as the manufacturer intended for that specific model to operate. Once you fail to maintain this ***harmony***, your circle will go out of balance and ***brake***.

Let us now examine the actions needed and the stations along our ***path to success and wealth***. Approach your process like growing a tree. Plant the seed, water it, take care of it, and watch it grow.

Enhance and Grow Your Awareness:

- **Meditate Daily:**

For at least thirty minute a day. Use guided meditation in your sessions, and ***make time for it***. Make sure you are not disturbed or distracted.

- **Write It Down:**

If you have any insights or ideas during your meditation, write them down afterwards, and review them in the context of your goals.

- **Focus:**

Focus on the ***present moment***, focus on what is happening around you, and draw the most of the current moment.

- **<u>Monitor Your Thoughts:</u>**

Don't submit to thoughts coming to your mind sporadically without examining and reviewing them. Have an *opinion.* If your opinion is that these thoughts are not contributing to your *mindset*, *dismiss them by interrupting their sequence and think of something productive.*

- **<u>Discipline Yourself:</u>**

Be aware of what *commitments* you took upon yourself. Write your commitments down, examine and evaluate yourself constantly. Once you detect that you strayed from your commitment, return directly to the course and try to understand what it was that took over your process instead of your plans.

- **<u>Be Present:</u>**

Whatever you do, whoever you are talking to, or whatever you are hearing or **saying** *(to others and to yourself)*, *Be Present.* If you find yourself drifting, then *consciously* pull yourself back to the moment.

<u>Imagination, Belief, and Desire:</u>

- **<u>Imagination</u>** is the most powerful tool we possess. Imagination defies the laws of physics and logic. It is the basis of *creativity* and *growth*. Imagination ignites initiative and feeds ambition. Practice imagination constantly, imagine the life you want to have, and see it as it has already been manifested and accomplished.

"Imagination is more important than knowledge. For knowledge is limited, whereas imagination embraces the entire world, stimulating progress, giving birth to evolution." (Albert

Einstein)

- **Be Ambitious:**

Always shoot for higher achievements. Don't be *satisfied* with what you have. Be *happy, and grateful* for what you have, but not satisfied. Satisfaction *kills* ambition, while imagination *fuels* it. Remember, there is no shortage of wealth or abundance in this world. There is more than enough for all.

- **Desire**:

Is the hidden force that helps us overcome difficulties and keep on going? A strong desire needs to accompany our imagination and ambitions. It is that force that will ensure us being tenacious to achieve our goals and dreams.

- **Believe:**

Nothing will be achieved if you don't believe in yourself, your ambitions, or your ability to achieve them. *The starting point* of your process is your *Belief.* If you are *half-hearted* towards yourself or your ambitions, or even worse, have no **Faith** in your ability to achieve them, then your efforts will be in vain. If you recognise a lack of Belief in yourself, start taking action to change that by following the steps discussed earlier in this book. Use affirmations and imagination, talk in the present tense, as if your goals are already achieved and enjoy the small wins along the way, for they will encourage your new beliefs.

"Believe you can and you're halfway there (Theodore Roosevelt)."

Think:

Thinking is the process of observing and analysing. It is the process of drawing conclusions from a given set of data. Thinking is *important* in order for us to evaluate the best course of action in a given situation. However, **overthinking** has the *opposite* results, and it is a process that leads to **doubts** and *fears*.

Think Methodically:

Adopt a systematic and organised way of thinking and executing. Practice thinking chronically, identifying cause and effect, and setting priorities. For example: since my years of executive management, I have developed a methodical thinking that helps me process and analyse data while receiving it. I see the data presented to me as diagrams and tables in my head, and I can intuitively identify correlations and relations between the parts of the information I am receiving. Methodical thinking is a sign of a high level of focus and helps organise thoughts and ideas in a practical manner.

Adopt Pausing Before Reacting:

Think before you react, answer, or state anything. Pause for ten seconds and talk. Weigh your words and make sure you understand the current situation before you react. In the beginning, in order to practice this, count until five and then react. If you think you didn't understand the situation at hand correctly, ask for clarifications before reacting or giving an opinion.

Reaction Vs Action:

Avoid being in the *reaction mode* all the time. To *react,* is to act in response to something that happened *to* you from outside, and over which you have no control or say in its occurrence. Push for *action*, this will place more *control* in your hands over situations.

Examine Your Environment:

Your environment is neither a given nor an unchangeable factor. Examine your environment and its influence on yourself and your achievements. Whatever is not aligned with and does not contribute to your ambitions and goals, *distance* yourself from it. Remember the wholeness of the circle, and the harmony needed in order to achieve your goals. Unsupportive environment, is a major cause of disharmony. Take charge, and *change* any environment that has no contribution to you.

"Stay away from negative people. They have a problem for every solution" (Albert Einstein).

Set Expectations:

When you start your journey and when you evaluate the priorities needed on your path, set expectations between you and your environment and between you and *yourself* for the allocation of resources. Setting expectations, will defuse possible clashes with your environment or with yourself. It will save a great deal of energy and crisis management and keep you focused on your path.

Seek Mentors:

In today's world, it is very easy to find and acquire a *mentor* in almost every domain of life. With the help of digital platforms, courses, and communities, the possibilities to enroll in a suitable plan that meets your needs are vast. The availability of mentoring on digital platforms also affecting the costs of the programmes and drastically reducing them. It is much cheaper to have a mentor who at the same time is engaging with 50 – 100 students (or more) than *one-on-one* mentoring. **Seek mentors** and learn from them, but before choosing a mentor, do your research carefully.

Change Unsupportive Habits and Beliefs:

Evaluate and *Examine* your habits. Understand what habits are pulling you back and which ones you need to strengthen or adopt all together. Identifying and changing *destructive* habits is a sign of *self-consciousness and courage*. Determine which habits you need to acquire, determine *how,* and *start* practicing. Don't *overwhelm* yourself, take it *gradually*, and proceed with step by step adjustment.

Repetition:

We can acquire new habits and new beliefs. This is a fact that is supported by numerous studies. Changing *habits* and *beliefs* is a process that takes time and effort. It is a conscious process that needs to be followed with a great deal of perseverance and determination. The secret to acquiring new habits and changing existing habits and beliefs, is rooted in the *Repetition* of the activity. *Repetition* enforces new neural pathways in our brain and makes them default patterns.

Ask for Advice:

If you fail to identify your faulty habits or beliefs, ask a close person to help you. This person needs to be *very close* and without any shadow of doubt, has *good intentions* for you and your *success*. It can be a good friend, a spouse, or a parent. If you find yourself asking for help, be *open-minded* and accept the opinions you hear. Sometimes it will not be easy and even surprising. Either way, you should listen and understand that if they say something that you don't feel or see, it doesn't mean that it isn't there. As we discussed before, this person can be your accountability partner who helps you stick to your plans.

Set Your Goals and Craft Your Plan of Action:
"Efforts and courage are not enough without purpose and direction" (JFK).

Set Your Goal:
After determining what it is that you want to achieve, set your **Goal**. The Goal needs to be clear and within a specified timeframe. The Goal cannot be without a deadline for achieving it, if so, then you will keep on postponing and lingering since there is no definite time to achieve what you set out to achieve. Furthermore, the Goal needs to be as specific in details as you can so it can be measurable. The Goal needs to be phrased in the present tense, as it's already been achieved. *For example: "By July next year, I added $50k to my yearly income."* You can also write the *"how"* if you want: *"By July next year, I added $50k to my yearly income, from my affiliate marketing business."* Don't limit your imagination, the higher you aim, the higher you will push.

Write It Down:
Write your goal down and place it in front of you all the time. Write it on a card and keep it with you, or, in a note on your phone. The constant exposure to the goal will motivate you in pursuing it and *"keep your eyes on the ball"*.

Set Your Plan:
Determine the plan of action that will get you to your goal. The plan is a set of multiple actions that need to take place in a

certain *order*, *quantity,* and *quality* in order to make an effective contribution to you in achieving your goal. The goal's achievement is an *aggregation* of all the executions of all of your tasks. You need to *write your plan down* in a *methodical* way, *specify* the *time* and *order* of execution for each task or group of tasks, and examine if they are connected to each other.

Take Immediate Action:

Once your plan is shaped, take immediate action. Even the smallest step in your plan is a step forward. Don't procrastinate. Take action!

"Things may come to those who wait but only the things left by those who hustle" (Abraham Lincoln).

Measure Your Performances:

Use tools to help you complete your tasks. You can use calendar events, "to-do" lists and written sticky notes if you use them. Whatever method helps you stick to your plan and complete your tasks, use it! *For me, for example,* works using calendars, notes on my phone, and to-do lists. I use each differently depending on the activity I want to monitor. Also, it would help a lot if you got in the habit of writing down your daily tasks and activities planned for the day, right after you finished your *meditation*, when you are focused and your mind is clear. Each following day, look at the previous day's tasks, examine which you have finished and which you haven't, and transfer unaccomplished tasks to the current day. Don't be harsh on yourself, and don't be judgmental for not finishing the tasks. Just accept it, observe it, and try to understand why you didn't finish what you committed yourself to, and try to avoid the reasons for it in the future.

Trust and Let Go:

"Letting go" of our **need to control** every outcome of our actions, is imperative in order for us to free ourselves from the anxiety and worry over the momentary results. Trust and let go means, that you believe that **God**, the **Universe,** or any **Devine higher force** you believe in, is looking after your best interests, as long as you fulfill your part of the *bargain*, and are Active, Confident, Believing in yourself and with the right Mindset. It is the highest level of faith, and you need to adopt it for your peace of mind and tranquility. Even more importantly, for you to be able to concentrate on pushing forward instead of *booting* in the same place. The *dynamics* of the *"moving parts"* in your plan, will almost never go exactly like you intended, but you need to Trust that it is going the right way. Freeing yourself from constant dealing with every small thing, will give you the ability to be *flexible* and adjust your plans, but, most importantly, it will give you the ability to see new *opportunities* evolving from the dynamics of things.

Be Flexible:

The previous step prepares you to be flexible. *Flexibility* in the *execution* of your plan is a *crucial ability* you should possess. *Flexibility* gives you the ability to change *priorities*, change a *thinking concept* or even change a complete *task* all together. ***Flexibility of Thought and Action***, gives you the confidence that even when the circumstances around you change, and do not support a certain effort any more, you know that your plan will not fall apart, since you know how to adjust it to the changing reality. And lastly, *Flexibility*, shows that you are *committed* and *tenacious* to your goal and *determined* to achieve it.

Don't Share Your Plan:

Never share your plans with anyone, not close or far. Except for your accountability partner or advisor, nobody should know about your plans. Discussing your plans with others will certainly expose you to some *discouraging* thoughts and advices. Those are not always *certified* opinions or given from an experienced point of view. Mostly, they will not always come from a *pure heart and good intentions*, but they will plant doubt in you and discourage you. Don't let your words explain your plans, make your actions speak for them.

Skills:

Enhance the skills you have or acquire new ones needed for you to achieve what you set out to achieve. Acquiring new skills is a quality you should have regardless of a certain plan, but even more so when they are needed for such a plan. Examine the things you do daily on automatic mode *(even as simple as brushing your teeth or mowing the grass in your garden)*. You are able to do these things without questioning your ability because you are *skilled* in doing them. The same for new skills, once you acquire them and practice them *Repeatedly*, they will become *trivial* and *normal* for you, and you will conduct them automatically.

Don't Be Afraid of Taking Risks:

"There are risks and costs to action. But they are far less than the long-range risks of comfortable inaction" (JFK).

Each action we take throughout our daily lives hides a certain *risk* in it, but we do it anyway. There is always a degree of *risk* that we are willing to take upon ourselves depending on the task at hand. Driving a car is *risky*, but yet we all drive anyway, taking a swim in the sea is *risky*, but we still enjoy doing so. Don't let the *risks* in your process pull you back. Understand the ***potential risks*** and evaluate, for yourself, what is an ***accepted risk*** for you. This is called a *"calculated risk"*, in which, you know what the price of failure is, and you are prepared to take it. To make a "calculated risk" acceptable to you, it needs to be **substantially smaller than the potential gain of your actions (your "Why")**.

Implement While Learning:

If your plan requires you to learn a new skill, that is perfect. You don't have to wait to be an expert in that skill in order for you to start. Once you started learning and got to a point where you can implement it, then, don't wait; implement while learning. It saves you time on the *"learning curve"*, and it gives you the ability to check your actions compared to the learning lessons. If you have a mentor, it would be very useful to implement the new skill you are acquiring while learning it. Since you can ask the questions raised from your own practical experience.

Face Your Fears:

At this point, different *fears* and *doubts* might invade your thoughts. Don't submit to them, and don't let your spirit break. Understand that it is ***normal*** and ***expected***. This is the reaction to change. The mind is playing its role as a ***survival mechanism***. ***Understand this, expect it, and deal with it.*** Face your fears and doubts *peacefully* and understand their origin, then remind yourself of your *absolute* certainty of your ***success,*** then release and dismiss your fears and doubts. Ignoring your fears will cost you dearly along the way, when your *resoluteness is much needed*.

"The only limit to our realization of tomorrow will be our doubts of today." (Franklin D. Roosevelt).

Be Grateful for What You Have:

"If you concentrate on what you don't have, you will never, ever have enough" (Oprah Winfrey).

Nothing in life is hundred per cent perfect. There is a bad opposed to every good, and vice versa. Our lives are not one-dimensional, and they are not constructed of one layer. Acknowledging the good things in your life *(life itself, family, health, wealth, relationships, sound mind, and etc.)* and being **Grateful** for having them is the right **mindset** for you to approach life with. **Give Gratitude** and appreciate the good things you have in life; they are taken for granted until they are missing. **Nothing is for granted;** while you are blessed with something, like health, for example, there are others who are less fortunate, and would sell all they have to be healthy. **Being Grateful** equips you with a **Positive Energy** that will keep you **balanced** and in **harmony**, and it will expand to all the other parts of your life as well, even those you see as missing.

Trade Money for Time:

As much as it is *possible* for your situation, try to **buy time with money**. What that means is that if you have the ability to hire an expert to do a task for you that you are not an expert in, it is *preferable* that you do so. It will save you the time of learning how to do that task, and *frees* you to invest the time in more *productive* aspects of executing your plan. This will also shorten your *"learning curve"*. Even if you know how to do something but you think it is time-consuming with a very weak *impact* on your achievement *(or for any other reason)*, I strongly advise you to *"outsource"* that task if you have the financial ability for it. The most *important* resource of all is **Time.** It is the only resource that *cannot be refilled*, once the Time is consumed, it is gone forever. Unlike Money and Energy that are *renewable* and can be *regenerated*. Utilizing time in a productive way, in which you *"are accounted for"* in each moment, is imperative for your success.

Practice Love Not Envy:

Love is one of the strongest forces in the universe. Our universe is built on the matter of *love*. Planet Earth and the Skies provide us with life and existence. Love the others, and wish them well and good fortune. Do not envy or badmouth them. Envy is a *destructive* force for you, as it is for the others, while *Love*, and is a life force that projects light and positive energy. If you embrace *Love* and renounce *Envy*, your positive energies will be *amplified,* and they will have *miraculous* impacts on your life and your *goals' achievements*.

Circulation of Money:

Money needs to be *circulated*. Money does not need to be stuffed in a mattress or even in a bank account. In order for money to produce money, it needs to circulate, it needs to be *invested,* and it needs to *return* to us *multiplied*. Money that is stuck away in some safe has no value since it is not doing anything, on the contrary, it is losing value because of inflation, economics, and other factors. When you have money, *invest it back in your business* or in Real Estate or any other business that can *yield* you more money. The power of money is in its *movement,* not *stillness*. Understand this, assess your options, and take *calculated risks* when investing your money. Investing money back in your business or in an asset will grow your money circulation and, at the same time, save you on taxes.

Passive Income:

The true form of wealth is **Passive Income**. *Passive income* sources are bringing you money without you actively putting in the time for it. Unlike *Active Income*, in which you need to invest time to earn money, **Passive Income** does not require your time to produce money, or at least the relative portion of your invested time will be *insignificant* compared to your benefit. Setting up a passive income business, may require you investing time in the beginning in order to make the business operational, but after the business is set up and running, it will produce for you income without any major effort on your part. Ideas for passive income can be: *Affiliate Marketing Business, Drop-Shipping, On Line Course, Writing a Book, Renting a Real Estate Property,* or *Selling Pictures Online, and etc.*

Multiple Sources of Income:

As much as you can, set yourself up with **Several Sources of Income,** and don't restrain yourself to one source only. The beauty and benefit of **Passive Income** businesses, is that they don't require much of your time, and they are relatively easy to set up. Furthermore, if one source of income is not producing any more or was hit by an unexpected difficulty *(for example, if you have a job and the company fired you)*, the other sources will still be generating income for you and **make up for the loss** of that first source. When **accumulated**, the incomes coming from many sources can make a big difference in your life and might be just the thing, that sets the **dividing line between being Wealthy or Poor**.